THE TEN COMMANDMENTS

THEN & NOW

THE TEN
COMMANDMENTS
THEN & NOW

ROBERT M. WEST

BARBOUR
PUBLISHING

Published by Barbour Publishing, Inc., P.O. Box 719, Uhrichsville, Ohio 44683, www.barbourbooks.com

Our mission is to publish and distribute inspirational products offering exceptional value and biblical encouragement to the masses.

Member of the
Evangelical Christian
Publishers Association

Printed in the United States of America.

Contents

*To my wife, Brenda, who has always been at my side in
learning, loving, and living the law of the Lord.*

INTRODUCTION

Let's travel back in time more than three thousand years to Mount Sinai—also called the Mountain of God—and consider how God came from heaven to meet with His chosen people, Israel, recently freed from centuries of slavery in Egypt.

He arrived in power and majesty. The people felt the mountain quake and saw it burn with fire as lightning flashed through a dark cloud. They heard a trumpet blast grow louder—and they were terrified.

God now had everyone's attention, and He gave them His law in an unforgettable way as He established a national covenant with Israel. The people agreed to obey, viewing God as the king of their new theocracy.

As a new nation, Israel needed laws to govern them. Having just been delivered from Egypt—a country filled with idols—the people were preparing to enter their "promised land." It was a good land, "flowing with milk and honey," which God had said He would give them. But it, too, had the potential to influence them toward idolatry.

Here and now, the Israelites needed to reestablish their relationship with the one true God and receive a national constitution to direct them. God would give them

- moral laws

- ceremonial laws, directing their worship of
  Him; and

- civil laws, addressing the affairs of their
  government and citizens.

These laws are found in the Bible, throughout the
books of Exodus, Leviticus, and Deuteronomy.

The Top Ten

The ancient Jews compiled more than six hundred
laws received from God—248 of them positive,
and 365 negative. But the major ones were the Ten
Commandments, also called the Decalogue ("ten
words"), which God gave to Moses on the mountain.

God spoke the Decalogue audibly, and with
His own finger engraved these laws on stone tablets
(Exodus 31:18; 32:15–16). Soon, these tablets were
broken by Moses, who was angry when the people
broke their agreement by worshipping a golden idol.
The Lord engraved a replacement set (Exodus 34:1,
28), which was stored in the Ark of the Covenant
(Deuteronomy 10:1–5) and served as a tangible
representation of God's law.

Centuries later, when Jesus was asked which
of the commandments was the greatest, He sum-

marized the ten into two inseparable rules—love the Lord your God with all your heart, soul, mind, and strength; and love your neighbor as yourself. These two principles formed the foundation of the entire law. Jesus said that loving God with all our hearts was the greatest commandment, and that loving our neighbors as ourselves was second (Matthew 22:36–40).

Jesus' answer shows how the Decalogue is divided: the first four commandments focus on the vertical, spiritual, relationship of loving God, and the remaining six focus on the horizontal, moral, relationship of loving other people. Thus, the Ten Commandments should be understood within the context of *love*.

The giving of the law was actually an act of kindness by God. Because the outcome of sin is always disastrous, the Bible states repeatedly that obedience to God's Word brings personal blessing. The Lord said to Moses, "Oh, that they had such a heart in them that they would fear Me and always keep all My commandments, *that it might be well with them* and with their children forever!" (Deuteronomy 5:29, emphasis added).

A Word of Caution

Some people mistakenly think that by doing their best to live by the Ten Commandments, they can earn their way into heaven. That's like getting wrong directions when traveling. They can follow them to the letter, but they'll end up in the wrong place. The apostle Paul initially made this mistake—as he zealously persecuted the new Christian church—but he eventually learned the true function of the law. In his writings, he presented the law's threefold purpose:

- The law shows people their *sin*. Paul writes, "By the law is the knowledge of sin" (Romans 3:20); and he also describes his experience: "I would not have known sin except through the law. For I would not have known covetousness unless the law had said, 'You shall not covet'" (Romans 7:7). Just as a mirror shows us what we're like on the outside, the law reveals the truth about our hearts.

- The law guides sinners to the *Savior* and His sacrificial death. "The law was our tutor to bring us to Christ, that we might be justified by faith" (Galatians 3:24). The law is a guardian, functioning through its system of sacrifices, symbols, prophecies, and pictures to direct people to the cross, where Jesus, as the

Lamb of God, died as a sacrifice for our sins.

• The law declares righteous *standards* that reflect the holy character of God. Moses said, "What great nation is there that has God so near to it. . .[and] has such statutes and righteous judgments as are in all this law?" (Deuteronomy 4:7–8). Paul called the law "holy and just and good" (Romans 7:12).

Performing religious works does not provide a ticket to heaven. Paul corrects this error three times in a single verse: "Knowing that a man is not justified by the works of the law but by faith in Jesus Christ, even we have believed in Christ Jesus, that we might be justified by faith in Christ and not by the works of the law; for by the works of the law no flesh shall be justified" (Galatians 2:16).

Salvation is never achieved by human effort or merit—only by personal trust in the person and work of Jesus Christ. Why? Because the law of God demands *absolute perfection*. Otherwise, it imposes a curse: "For as many as are of the works of the law are under the curse; for it is written, 'Cursed is everyone *who does not continue in all things* which are written in the book of the law, to do them'" (Galatians 3:10, emphasis added).

Perfection? Who can achieve perfection? The truth is that no one can ever be good enough to earn salvation—because if we break even one commandment, we're guilty of the entire law and under the law's curse (James 2:10). Only Christ was sinless (1 Peter 2:22), never breaking a commandment of God's. What a joy it must have been for Paul to write these words: "Christ has redeemed us from the curse of the law" (Galatians 3:13). To become children of God, all we need to do is trust in the work of Jesus—His perfect life, sacrificial death, and resurrection; "for 'the just shall live by faith'" (Galatians 3:11).

The issue is really quite simple: We either trust in ourselves and offer our works to God; or we trust in Jesus and what He has done, as our only hope for salvation.

Why Study the Ten Commandments?

Christians understand that distinct differences exist between the Old and New Testaments, differences that might discourage their study. The following shows that the law of Moses has ended and been replaced:

- "The law was given through Moses, but grace and truth came through Jesus Christ" (John 1:17). Throughout time, God's revelation to men has been gradual. The law of Moses, which was preparatory, contained grace and truth, but this revelation was limited—like dim moonlight. The coming of Christ and His complete revelation of grace and truth was like the brilliant sun light.

- The one sacrifice of Jesus Christ dying on the cross culminates what the Old Testament animal sacrifices only shadowed (Hebrews 10:1–4, 11–14).

- The Old Testament priesthood has been replaced by the Great High Priest, Jesus Christ (Hebrews 7:11–12; 4:14–16).

- The old covenant was temporary, with a built-in expiration date; but a new covenant, with better promises, was provided by God through Jesus Christ (Hebrews 7:17–22; 8:6–13; 2 Corinthians 3:7–11).

Having said all this, we must remember that God's moral law is timeless—it applies to all ages. It has been written in stone, as well as on our hearts. God's moral law didn't begin at Mount Sinai. Moses said that Abraham, who lived more than five hundred years before the Decalogue was given, kept God's commandments (Genesis 26:5). For their part, New Testament authors repeatedly quoted the Old Testament to strengthen their exhortations, showing that New Testament morality is built upon Old Testament morals. In 1 Peter 1:15, Peter quoted Leviticus 11:44–45 to encourage Christians to live holy lives.

In our day, society's moral boundaries are being moved. Our nation has returned to the lifestyle of the days of the judges, when "everyone did what was right in his own eyes" (Judges 21:25). For many, the Ten Commandments have become the Ten Opinions. Violating and mocking God's law has become so common that Hollywood makes it a form of entertainment. Politicians add to the decay by legalizing sin. But the Ten Commandments, written in stone, stand as the anchor for morality by revealing God's standard regarding right and wrong. The church, as "the salt of the earth" and "the light of the world," must not waver.

The concern of this book is to be *biblically* correct rather than politically correct. God has preserved His law in the Bible, for our benefit today. That's why we study the Ten Commandments.

Fulfilling the Law

A recent news headline is both humorous and troubling: Survey: More Americans Familiar with Big Mac Ingredients than Ten Commandments. Clearly, we have some work to do. We must first *learn* the law if we are to know how to apply it.

Nine of the ten commandments are restated in the New Testament and clearly apply to Christian living. And since all scripture is profitable (2 Timothy 3:16), the aim of the following chapters will be to consider lessons from all ten of the commandments God handed down to Moses.

The apostle Paul clearly valued the law: "We know that the law is good if one uses it properly" (1 Timothy 1:8 NIV). And because Jesus came to *fulfill* the law (Matthew 5:17), a study of the Ten Commandments can reveal truths to encourage us, challenge us, and build us up in our faith.

As Paul discussed victory over the power and pollution of sin in the Christian life, he said that the law, as a mere list of rules, provides no power to help us overcome sin. But our being under grace—through our union with Christ—means that an enabling power is provided for victory (Romans 6:14). A poet put it like this:

> *Do this and live the law commands*
>   *but gives me neither feet nor hands.*
> *A sweeter sound the gospel brings,*
>   *it bids me fly and gives me wings.*

Through God's grace, let's have God's laws written on our hearts and displayed in our lives for our own blessing, the good of others, and the glory of God.

> *Free from the law, O happy condition,*
> *Jesus has bled and there is remission.*
> *Cursed by the law and bruised by the fall,*
> *Grace has redeemed us once for all.*

PHILIP P. BLISS, "ONCE FOR ALL" (1873)

Discussion Questions

1. How many of the Ten Commandments can you state?
2. What is the greatest commandment?
3. What are three purposes of the law?
4. What is the one thing the law can't do?

1

THE FIRST COMMANDMENT: GOD AND GOD ALONE

"You shall have no other gods before Me."

EXODUS 20:3

As the Ten Commandments begin, God claims an exclusive right to be acknowledged as the only one to be worshipped. We are to have no other gods in addition to Him.

God placed this commandment at the beginning as foundational to the others. A proper relationship with God begins with His preeminence and extends to all of life. When we get this commandment right, the rest can fall into place.

Both the Old and New Testaments begin with the devil tempting people to break this commandment. In Genesis, Satan tells Eve that she will become like God if she will eat the forbidden fruit. When she and Adam give in to this temptation, sin enters the world (Genesis 3:1–6).

In the Gospel of Matthew, as Jesus prepares for His public ministry, the devil tempts Him to replace

His trust in the plan of God with trust in what the devil could provide if Jesus worshipped *him*. Jesus rebuffs this temptation (Matthew 4:8–11). Today, nothing has changed. The enemy of our souls still tempts us to fill our lives with everything but God.

The God of the Old Testament

Who is this God that says, "Have no other gods before *Me*"? In Exodus 20:2, the preface of the Decalogue, He describes Himself and His unique relationship to Israel:

- "I am the Lord. . ." When the term Lord appears in all capital letters in English Bibles, it refers to God's name Yahweh or Jehovah, which means "the God who is." It is connected to the mysterious name "I AM WHO I AM" that God used in revealing His changeless self-existence to Moses (Exodus 3:14). It is God's personal and special covenant name to Israel.

- "your God. . ." He is the God of relationships, whose covenant with Israel begins with His gracious call of Abraham in Genesis 12.

- "who brought you out of the land of Egypt,

out of the house of bondage." He is the Redeemer, who set His people free from slavery by His power and by the sacrificial blood of the Passover lamb.

This reminder of who God is and what He has done for Israel was to encourage His people to love and obey Him.

THE FIRST COMMANDMENT— THEN

Israel understood that there were at least four things that God was prohibiting:

- *Atheism.* Though virtually nonexistent at the time of Moses, atheism is the belief that God does not exist. God says, "The fool has said in his heart, 'There is no God'" (Psalm 14:1).

- *Idolatry.* Idolatry is worshipping a false god in place of the Lord. God has said that no other gods exist. "Thus says the LORD, the King of Israel, and his Redeemer, the LORD of hosts: I am the First and I am the Last; besides Me there is no God. . . . Is there a God besides Me? . . . I know not one" (Isaiah 44:6, 8).

- *Polytheism.* Polytheists worship many false gods simultaneously. They believe that different gods exist for different purposes, and that they are to be worshipped to receive specific benefits. The numerous Egyptian gods were targets of the Lord's judgment (Exodus 12:12).

- *Syncretism.* Syncretism is the worship of false gods and the LORD together, as if they are of equal standing. While Moses spent weeks on Mount Sinai receiving the law from God, his brother Aaron led the people in worshipping a golden calf idol and the LORD at the same time (Exodus 32:1–5). Though Israel had been taken out of Egypt, it wasn't easy to take the legacy of four hundred years in Egypt out of Israel.

The first commandment is presented in negative terms, indicating what should *not* be done. Just as parents will say no to their children for their own good, God does the same. Nevertheless, each commandment, including the first commandment, has two sides—a positive and a negative. The positive side of this commandment is that people should develop their love for God. "Hear, O Israel: The

LORD our God, the LORD is one! You shall love the LORD with all your heart, with all your soul, and with all your strength" (Deuteronomy 6:4–5).

Idolatry was a problem throughout Israel's history, until God finally purged it from their midst through the judgment of the Babylonian captivity. Its outward expressions then vanish from scripture's historical record, though only to be replaced by accounts of other national sins.

THE FIRST COMMANDMENT—NOW

Moses had limited information about God, because God chose to reveal Himself gradually throughout scripture. Since the coming of Christ and the completion of the New Testament, however, there has been significant advancement in God's revelation of Himself and what we are to believe about Him.

The God of the New Testament

God has revealed that He exists as one God in three eternal and equal persons in the Godhead. Christianity calls this the Holy Trinity: God the Father, God the Son, and God the Holy Spirit. The word *trinity* isn't found in the Bible, but its truth is established in the following ways.

- Each Person—Father, Son, and Spirit—is called *God* (1 Corinthians 8:6; Hebrews 1:8; Acts 5:3–4).

- Each Person has the same divine attributes—for example, eternal existence (Romans 16:26; John 8:58; Hebrews 9:14).

- Each Person does the same divine work— for example, the salvation of sinners (1 Peter 1:1–2).

- Each Person is referred to in the formula of Christian baptism (Matthew 28:19).

- Each Person is named in the use of benedictions (2 Corinthians 13:14).

"Who Do Men Say That I Am?"

When Jesus asked His disciples this question, Simon Peter gave the correct answer: "You are the Christ the Son of the living God" (Matthew 16:16). Because Jesus is "the fullness of the Godhead bodily," and the One who died for sinners, He is the object of faith in the gospel message (John 3:16–18; Colossians 2:9).

Jesus also identified Himself as Jehovah of the Old Testament when He said, "Most assuredly I say to you, before Abraham was, I AM" (John 8:58; see also Exodus 3:14). The Jewish leaders swiftly rejected Christ's claim of equality with God, accusing Him of blasphemy deserving of death (John 8:59; 10:30–33).

It should not be overlooked that Jesus accepted worship from His followers without admonishing them that they were breaking the first commandment (John 9:35–38; 20:28). In contrast, holy angels refused worship (Revelation 19:10; 22:8–9). Paul and Barnabas also resisted adulation (Acts 14:12–15), but Jesus accepted it. Though His enemies opposed Him, His disciples worshipped Him.

Violating the First Commandment Today

If you think that idolatry is a thing of the past because we aren't dancing around golden idols, consider this: One form of idolatry today is worshipping ourselves, other people, and our material possessions instead of worshipping God.

Paul exhorted Christians to rid from their lives "covetousness, which is idolatry" (Colossians 3:5). Covetousness is the sin of greed, of always wanting more, which is a form of idolatry. Many people have replaced God in their lives with worship of the human trinity: me, myself, and I. Their prayer is, "*My* kingdom come, *my* will be done." These people act as if the world revolves around them as they seize God's place.

All Roads Lead to God?

Is it true—as many people believe—that other world religions worship the same God, but under different names? By examining the beliefs of some major world faiths, we can see that it's not true.

- *Hindus* worship Brahma, an impersonal god manifested in more than 300,000 gods and goddesses.
- *Muslims* worship their one god, Allah, who would never be incarnate.
- *Buddhists* generally do not believe in a god and focus on human enlightenment.
- *Christians* worship God, who is One in three Persons, the Holy Trinity, who became incarnate in the Person of the Lord Jesus Christ, the "King of kings and Lord of lords." He stands alone by virtue of His virgin birth, sinless life, sacrificial death, and resurrection from the dead.

In the "last days," the apostle Paul said, the first commandment will be ignored. "Men will be lovers of themselves, lovers of money. . . unloving. . .lovers of pleasure rather than lovers of God" (2 Timothy 3:2–4).

Christians are warned to beware of people who could be a bad influence—"whose god is their belly . . .who set their mind on earthly things" (Philippians 3:19). These idolaters make a god out of their own appetites, believing that life's highest good is to please themselves. Their motto is, "He who dies with the most toys wins."

Keeping the First Commandment Today

To keep the first commandment today, we must acknowledge Jesus Christ alone as the God whom we worship and serve. Jesus made an exclusive claim when He said, "I am the way, the truth, and the life. No one comes to the Father except through Me" (John 14:6).

After Pentecost, the apostle Peter was arrested and interrogated about his politically incorrect preaching. He responded by affirming the power and name of Jesus Christ, and said, "Nor is there salvation in any other, for there is no other name under heaven given among men by which we must be saved" (Acts 4:12).

Paul commended the Thessalonians because they

had "turned to God from idols to serve the living and true God" (1 Thessalonians 1:9).

The positive side of this commandment also teaches that Christ is to be our number one love in life. When addressing this subject with the doctrinally sound Ephesian church, Christ expressed His displeasure by saying, "I have this against you, that you have left your first love" (Revelation 2:4). The Ephesians were so busy working *for* Jesus that they neglected to spend time *with* Him. His counsel to them is still good today:

- *"Remember from where you have fallen. . ."* Jesus admonished them to think back and pinpoint where the problem began of letting other things interfere with their love for Him.

- *"repent. . ."* The Ephesians were called to have a humble change of mind and heart about their love for Christ, which had grown cold.

- *"and do the first works."* They were to return to and *repeat* what they had formerly done to cultivate a growing love for the Lord (Revelation 2:4–5).

The first commandment teaches us that the Lord Jesus Christ is to be God and God alone in our lives. He is to be our ultimate priority and our first love.

> *Immortal, invisible, God only wise,*
> *In light inaccessible hid from our eyes,*
> *Most blessed, most glorious,*
>   *the Ancient of Days,*
> *Almighty, victorious,*
> *Thy great name we praise.*

WALTER CHALMERS SMITH, "IMMORTAL, INVISIBLE" (1839)

Discussion Questions

1. Why is this commandment placed at the beginning of the Decalogue?
2. How does God reveal Himself in the New Testament?
3. Do people in different religions actually worship the same God?
4. How do people break this commandment today?

2

THE SECOND COMMANDMENT: AN EXTREME MAKEOVER

"You shall not make for yourself a carved image."
EXODUS 20:4

Reality shows about extreme makeovers of homes, women's appearance, and weight loss, have captivated their viewing audiences.

The second commandment is also about an extreme makeover—in religion. Here, people are called to refrain from producing images that misrepresent what God is really like. Instead, we're to worship the one true God in the proper way—which is without images. Images are used to worship false gods, and thus God does not want them used to worship Him. True worship must have a spiritual emphasis, not a material emphasis, which can lead to idolatry. As the Creator of all things, God reserves the right to tell His people how He wants to be worshipped.

The Reasons for This Prohibition

The human issue. As humans, we have a tendency to worship idols. Even Israel, the people of God, were guilty of worshipping the bronze serpent image that God had instructed Moses to make as a solution to divine judgment (Numbers 21:4–9; 2 Kings 18:4).

The divine issue. The story is told of a kindergarten teacher who asked a young boy what he was drawing. He said, "A picture of God." The teacher smiled and said, "But nobody knows what God looks like." The boy put down the crayon and looked at her and said, "They will when I'm done!"

There is no image that can accurately represent our infinite God without tarnishing His true character. Consider the following:

- *God is alive, but statues are not.* Israel was taunted by its pagan neighbors because its God could not be seen. The Jews responded by comparing the sovereign heavenly God to lifeless man-made earthly images: "Their idols are silver and gold, the work of men's hands. They have mouths, but they do not speak; eyes they have, but they do not see; they have ears, but they do not hear; noses they have, but they do not smell; they have hands, but they do not handle; feet they have, but they do not walk; nor do they mutter through their throat. Those who make them are like them; so is everyone who trusts in them" (Psalm 115:4–8).

- *God is infinite, but images are finite.* It is impossible to represent the unlimited nature of God with anything tangible. (2 Chronicles 6:18).

- *God's formlessness.* God revealed Himself to Israel on Mount Sinai without a form; thus, the people shouldn't be tempted to make images of Him (Deuteronomy 4:15–24). His presence was verbal, not visible, as He spoke the Ten Commandments.

    Moses later asked God to reveal His glory visually (Exodus 33:18), but God told him, "You cannot see My face; for no man shall see Me, and live" (Exodus 33:20). Moses was permitted to see a vision of limited glory and hear God extol His moral attributes (Exodus 33:20–23). The prophet Isaiah, realizing that nothing created can accurately represent God, asks, "To whom then will you liken God? Or what likeness will you compare to Him?" (Isaiah 40:18).

Idols come in all shapes and sizes.

Paul said that idolaters "changed the glory of the incorruptible God into an image made like corruptible man—and birds and four-footed animals and creeping things" (Romans 1:23).

One of the seven wonders of the ancient world was the Colossus of Rhodes. This statue of the Greek sun god Helios was almost as tall as the Statue of Liberty in New York City.

King Nebuchadnezzar's golden image was ninety feet tall. Three Jews—Shadrach, Meshach, and Abed-Nego—were thrown into a fiery furnace because they would not violate the second commandment by bowing down to the image of the king (Daniel 3).

Rachel, who came from a pagan family, hid her father's small household idols in a camel's saddle-bag. Her husband, Jacob, eventually got rid of them by burying them in the ground (Genesis 31:19; 35:4).

THE SECOND COMMANDMENT— THEN

The Jews understood that they were not to manufacture images of any kind for the purpose of worshipping God. God's instructions in Exodus 20:4 covered objects from three categories of creation— anything in the heavens, on earth, or in the sea.

The purpose of God's creation was to reflect His glory, not to misrepresent Him as something finite. King David said, "The heavens declare the glory of God; and the firmament shows His handiwork" (Psalm 19:1). Paul writes, "For all that may be known of God by men lies plain before their eyes; indeed God himself has disclosed it to them. His invisible attributes, that is to say his everlasting power and deity, have been made visible, ever since the world began, to the eye of reason, in the things he has made" (Romans 1:19–20 NEB).

Artistry Was Not Prohibited

This commandment did not prohibit the making of *all* images, for God empowered artisans and gave them instructions about how to make the following objects:

- Statues of cherubim were placed on the

Ark of the Covenant in the holy of holies (Exodus 25:18–20).

- Pictures of cherubim were also embroidered on the veil of the tabernacle (Exodus 26:1).

- The massive water basin in Solomon's temple was placed on twelve large statues of oxen (1 Kings 7:23–25).

- Moses made a bronze serpent and put it on a pole for the people to look at in order to be healed from a judgment of poisonous snakebites (Numbers 21:8–9).

Though certain images were made for other purposes, there was no image that could accurately represent God. The point of the prohibition had to do with the problem of idolatry, not artistry, as indicated by the rest of the commandment, which says, "You shall not bow down to them nor serve them" (Exodus 20:5).

Reasons That Encourage Obedience

An extended section is attached to this commandment in Exodus 20:5–6 that explains why it should be obeyed. In it, God reveals three things about Himself and His actions.

- *God is jealous.* This can be misunderstood, because the Bible says that "jealousy is the rage of a man" (Proverbs 6:34 KJV) and "jealousy is cruel as the grave" (Song of Solomon 8:6 KJV). But God is not sinful, He's holy. His intense love and devotion for His people is called "godly jealousy" in 2 Corinthians 11:2. It isn't that God is *jealous* of other false gods, but He is *zealous* to protect what is His. It is a jealousy that rightly refuses to share His people with another god. This same godly jealousy is seen in families where husbands and wives are devoted to each other and where parents are devoted to their children. God's devotion and love are so much a part of who He is that the Bible calls him "the LORD, whose name is Jealous" (Exodus 34:14).

- *God is a judge.* Here is a warning: God says that He "visit[s] the iniquity of the fathers upon the children to the third and fourth generation of those who hate Me" (Exodus 20:5). This is a way of saying that God, in His holiness, gives people what they deserve for their iniquity. The sad reality is

that our sin affects other people. A cycle
of sin can be put in motion as a parent's
sinful example influences future generations
to become disobedient God haters like
their forefathers. Still, Deuteronomy
24:16 makes it clear that all people are
accountable for their own actions.

- *God is merciful.* What a contrast to the
preceding verse! Though God will punish
those who oppose Him, He grants mercy
to those who love Him and keep His
commandments. Before, there was hatred
of God; now there is love and obedience.
Before, there was judgment from God; now
there's mercy. Instead of a few generations
receiving the curse, now thousands receive
the blessing.

THE SECOND COMMANDMENT— NOW

The point of the second commandment runs much
deeper than just the elimination of idols from
outward worship. The Lord saw that some of His
people had erected idols in their hearts, as well. By
doing this they were inwardly turning away from

God, even though outwardly they claimed to follow Him. Idolatry of the heart is like the early stages of a disease that must be treated quickly before it gets worse (Ezekiel 14:1–8).

False Images of God

Idols manufactured in a person's mind lead to a faulty view of God, one that supersedes what God has revealed about Himself in scripture. John Calvin said man's nature "is a perpetual factory of idols." People prefer a God who is always tolerant, loving, understanding, and forgiving—in other words, a God who forgoes judgment and never condemns. This is like saying, "Let us make God in our own image."

Even the strongest of Christians, during times of deep adversity, are tempted to question God's wisdom, faithfulness, and love. Who among us, when facing life's challenges, hasn't cried out with Gideon, "If the LORD is with us, why then has all this happened to us?" (Judges 6:13). But any false images of God in our hearts must be destroyed.

Images of God That He Has Made

Only God can make images of Himself, and He has done this in the following ways:

- *Adam and Eve were created in the image*

of God (Genesis 1:26–27). God created Adam and Eve in His image, which is what separates humans from animals. The likeness of God includes our rational, moral, and spiritual qualities. As rational beings, we have intellect, emotion, and will—like God. As moral beings, we are able to share in God's communicable attributes, such as love, integrity, and wisdom. As spiritual beings, we have an eternal spirit with the capacity to have fellowship with God. Because of sin, however, this image was distorted and corrupted.

- *Jesus Christ is the perfect image of God* (Colossians 1:15). Paul says that Christ is the exact representation of God—not *created,* but the very image of God. Though God is invisible, we can find out what He's like by getting to know the Lord Jesus. Jesus said, "He who has seen Me has seen the Father" (John 14:9). The invisible God has become visible through His Son.

- *Christians are being made into the image of God* (Colossians 3:10). Because believers in Christ are "new creations," they are to be involved in a daily renewal process of becoming more Christlike. Warren Wiersbe puts it well: "We were *formed* in God's image, and *deformed* from God's image by sin. But through Jesus Christ, we can be *transformed* into God's image!"

It is said that on a wall near the main entrance of the Alamo in San Antonio, Texas, is a portrait with the following inscription: "James Butler Bonham—no picture of him exists. This portrait is of his nephew, Major James Bonham, deceased, who greatly resembled his uncle. It is placed here by the family that people may know the appearance of the man who died for freedom."

No portrait or image of Christ exists, but His likeness is to be seen in the lives of His followers. We need an extreme makeover spiritually! We aren't to make lifeless images of God, but we are to become living images of God as He transforms our lives.

> *The dearest idol I have known*
> *What ere' that idol be,*
> *Help me to tear it from Thy throne*
> *And worship only Thee.*

WILLIAM COWPER, "O FOR A CLOSER WALK WITH GOD" (1769)

Discussion Questions

1. How is this commandment different from the first one?
2. What is the problem of using images to worship?
3. What are the three stated reasons in this commandment encouraging obedience?
4. What images has God made of Himself?

3

THE THIRD COMMANDMENT:
BLESSED BE THE NAME
OF THE LORD

*"You shall not take the name of the LORD
your God in vain, for the LORD will not hold
him guiltless who takes His name in vain."*

EXODUS 20:7

It was a common in Bible times to give names based
on their meaning. The first man was named *Adam,*
meaning "earthy," because he was made from the
dust of the ground. The first woman was named
Eve, meaning "life," because she was "the mother
of all living" (Genesis 3:20). When the Son of God
became incarnate, He was named *Jesus,* which means
"Jehovah saves," because He would "save His people
from their sins" (Matthew 1:21).

Today, our names may not be tied to particular
attributes, but they can take on a certain significance
based on our character and reputation. Credit card
companies associate our name with how we use
credit. Doctors and dentists relate our name to how

we take care of ourselves. Employers connect our name with our work ethic, and so on.

Pastor Alistair Begg tells the humorous story of a lawyer whose name was Odd. All through his life, people made fun of him, saying, "You're really odd," or calling him "Oddball." When he created his last will and testament, he gave specific instructions not to put his name on the tombstone. Instead, he wanted the inscription, "Here lies an honest lawyer." After his death, people walking through the cemetery would see the inscription and say, "An honest lawyer? That's odd!"

It's commonly thought that the third commandment simply prohibits using God's name as profanity. Although that's certainly included, much more is involved. Generally speaking, God is concerned that He receive the honor due His name. The issue is not just *using* God's name, but *abusing* it. Arthur W. Pink said, "His name must not be used with contempt, irreverently, or needlessly. In our speech, nothing must enter that lowers the divine dignity of that Name."

> *"You must not misuse the name*
> *of the LORD your God."*
> EXODUS 20:7 NLT

God's Name

A single name for God could not reflect the total significance of His nature and character, so He reveals Himself in many names. The Old Testament records His three primary names or titles:

- *Elohim* (translated "God") reveals Him as the strong and faithful Creator ("In the beginning God created..." Genesis 1:1)

- *Yahweh* or *Jehovah* (translated "Lord") reveals Him as eternally self-existent ("Lord Most High over all the earth" Psalm 83:18).

- *Adonai* (translated "Lord") reveals Him as a master ("God of gods and Lord of lords" Deuteronomy 10:17).

Often in scripture, when the Lord proclaims His own name, rather than giving a particular name, He describes His character: "The Lord God, merciful and gracious, longsuffering, and abounding in goodness and truth, keeping mercy...forgiving...by no means clearing the guilty" (Exodus 34:6–7).

The Bible includes many names for God, but the greatest name by which He is known is Lord Jesus Christ.

Here is the beginning of an
alphabetical list of Jesus' names
that I encourage you to complete
as you study the Bible:

Almighty   Revelation 1:8
Bread of Life   John 6:35
Chief Cornerstone   Ephesians 2:20
Door   John 10:9
Everlasting Father   Isaiah 9:6

THE THIRD COMMANDMENT—
THEN

God's name, which represents who He is and what He's like, includes many different names that are always to be held in high esteem. Specific instructions were given for the proper use of God's name. These instructions included both prohibitions and proper usages.

What the Old Testament Prohibits

- *Confirming a lie or breaking a vow* (Leviticus 19:12). When invoking God's name, wedding vows should not be broken. In courtrooms, perjury should never be committed. Business agreements should not be broken. In private matters, too many have said, "I promise not to tell!" and then later spread gossip.

- *Speaking against God* (Psalm 139:20). God's enemies at times blame Him for life's calamities and criticize Him for the way He runs the world that He made. Even Job's sorrowful wife tempted him to curse God, who she believed was at fault for their trouble and loss.

- *Doubting God's care* (Proverbs 30:8–9).
  Extreme circumstances of wealth or poverty
  involve moral dangers. In wealth comes the
  temptation to arrogance and self-reliance,
  forgetting God's providence. In poverty,
  some people become angry with God,
  forsake trusting Him, and resort to theft,
  which ruins the person's reputation and
  brings reproach on God's name.

- *Being a poor testimony* (Ezekiel 36:20–23).
  People tend to view God through the
  actions of His people. This is guilt by
  association. In the book of Ezekiel,
  God's promises were questioned because
  disobedient Israel was forced out of the
  Promised Land. God later restored the
  Jews to their land and to Himself—thereby
  demonstrating to unbelievers that His word
  can be trusted.

- *Speaking God's name carelessly* (Exodus
  20:7). What does it mean to "take God's
  name *in vain*"? The phrase "in vain" means
  empty, useless, and without thought. So
  using God's name in vain means to invoke
  His name in passing without a worthy

reason. Many people speak God's name irreverently so often that they are unaware that they have even mentioned His blessed name.

A Warning

Once again, to encourage obedience in God's standards, a warning is attached to the end of this commandment, revealing how serious God is about His name: "For the Lord will not hold him guiltless who takes His name in vain." But because often there is no immediate and devastating consequence when someone breaks this commandment, many people disregard the warning. Nevertheless, God does hold people accountable who have sinned against His name (Matthew 12:34–37).

What the Old Testament Promotes

Though this commandment is phrased as a prohibition, elsewhere in scripture we find positive examples of how to use God's name in an honorable way:

- *Trust in God.* "Those who know Your name will put their trust in You" (Psalm 9:10). God does not forsake those who seek His help in times of trouble. Those who know Him realize that they can put their trust in Him.

- *Personal worship.* "All that is within me, bless His holy name!" (Psalm 103:1). King David learned that true praise must come from the heart, involve total concentration, be focused on the Lord, and engage his memory. For him, such praise was real soul music!

- *Corporate worship.* "Oh, magnify the LORD with me, and let *us* exalt His name *together*" (Psalm 34:3, emphasis added). The fruit of personal worship will spill over to others and become a chorus of praise. The goal of this joint endeavor is that the Lord's name will get all the attention and increase in fame and influence.

THE THIRD COMMANDMENT—
NOW

It is important to understand that this commandment can be broken in ways other than *speaking* God's name irreverently. His name, which represents His attributes, authority, and actions, is to be used only in ways that honor Him.

The New Testament adds additional prohibitions and lessons to those found in the Old Testament. In addition to respecting the name of God, we're also called to honor the name of Jesus Christ.

TV as Teacher?

The Parents Television Council reports that in 2007, the most recent year for which they have data, 95.9% of uses of the word *God* on primetime network television were in vain.

What the New Testament Prohibits

The New Testament warns against both careless and presumptuous use of the Lord's name.

- *Using God's name in profanity* (Colossians 3:5–8). Christians are to be actively involved in developing Christlike behavior, which includes watching how we talk. Blasphemy and filthy language must be banished in favor of praise and edifying conversation.

- *Using the Lord's name hypocritically* (Matthew 7:21–23). Some people give the appearance of being genuine believers— giving lip service to Christ and doing religious works—but something is missing. The Lord can see that His name is not truly written in their hearts by faith.

What the New Testament Promotes

Honoring God's name involves several aspects of faith, speech, and lifestyle.

- *Having faith in Christ* (John 20:30–31). "Believing on His name" to receive eternal life includes personally trusting what the scriptures reveal about who Jesus is and what He's done. The experience of "doubting Thomas" illustrates this (John 20:24–29).

- *Honoring God's name in prayer* (Matthew 6:9). Jesus taught His disciples certain priorities in prayer. We should always begin with our focus on God and the honor He deserves for who He is. Sometimes we are so preoccupied with ourselves that we focus our prayers on selfish requests. Honoring the name of our heavenly Father will help us keep our priorities straight.

- *Praying in Jesus' name* (John 16:23–24). Jesus promises that God the Father will grant our requests when we pray *in His name*. But what does it mean to pray in Jesus' name? The words "in Jesus' name" are not a magic incantation, as the exorcists in Acts 19 found out, something to be added to the end of a prayer to guarantee God's acceptance. Prayer in Jesus' name means that we identify with Christ in His cause, will, and glory. To intentionally omit the name of Jesus from prayer is to sacrifice God's acceptance of a prayer.

- *Speaking with honesty* (James 5:12). It was an ancient Jewish custom to swear by heaven and earth to make one's words believable but not actually binding. But to use God's name in an oath made it binding. Even today you'll hear someone say, "I cross my heart," or "I swear by my mother's grave," or "I swear to God." Christians, however, should be honest and trustworthy at all times and have no need for swearing oaths.

- *Living a life of holiness* (2 Timothy 2:19). Those who confess faith in Christ, who was without sin and died to save us from our sins, must leave behind their old, sinful lives. Genuine faith is seen in lives that strive to obey God. The importance of having one's conduct match his or her confession is illustrated in the following story:

    In the army of Alexander the Great, a soldier who was also named Alexander was accused of cowardly actions. When he was brought before Alexander, the king asked for his name. He replied softly, "Alexander." "I can't hear you!" the ruler said. The man said again, a little louder, "Alexander." The process was repeated a third time, after which Alexander the Great said, "Either change your conduct or change your name!"

For those who love the blessed name of the Lord, it is good to know that the day is coming when blasphemy, irreverence, and mocking will cease. In that day, "at the name of Jesus, every knee [will] bow . . .every tongue [will] confess that Jesus Christ is Lord, to the glory of God the Father" (Philippians 2:10–11).

> *I praise Thee, Lord, for cleansing me from sin.*
> *Fulfill Thy word and make me pure within.*
> *Fill me with fire where once I burned with*
>   *shame.*
> *Grant my desire to magnify Thy name.*
>   J. EDWIN ORR, "CLEANSE ME" (1936)

Discussion Questions

1. Why was the Christ child named Jesus?
2. What are the meanings of the three primary names of God?
3. What positive lessons can we glean from this commandment?
4. Which name of Jesus has special meaning for you? Why?

4

THE FOURTH COMMANDMENT: TIMEOUT!

"Remember the Sabbath day, to keep it holy."
EXODUS 20:8

Taking a "timeout" is a common experience. For example, many sports allow timeouts in order for teams to regroup, catch their breath, and adjust their strategies. Employers provide break times, lunchtime, and vacation time away from work. Some cultures make time for daily afternoon siestas, when businesses close for two or three hours.

The fourth commandment prescribes a weekly timeout during which God's people were to abstain from work. The word *Sabbath* means "to cease from activity." In ancient Israel, the Sabbath was a day set aside to rest from the toil of work and to worship God.

This commandment affects our use of time. The devil wants to squeeze God out of our lives by tempting us to busyness. He wants us to view our "personal time" as vital and our time with God as optional. But God wants us to understand that time spent with Him is essential and valuable.

Our worship should strive to reflect the worship taking place in Heaven, where the angels and those of God's people who have gone on before us live to honor and adore God. Consider the words of the twenty-four elders worshipping in heaven: "Thou art worthy, O Lord, to receive glory and honor and power: for thou hast created all things, and for thy pleasure they are and were created" (Revelation 4:11 KJV).

THE FOURTH COMMANDMENT— THEN

The Lord gave Israel an entire sabbatical system as a testimony to their relationship with Him. Just like wedding rings are a sign of marriage, the Sabbath was a symbol of God's covenant relationship with Israel. "Surely My Sabbaths you shall keep, for it is a sign between Me and you throughout your generations, that you may know that I am the LORD who sanctifies you" (Exodus 31:13). Israel was to keep this day special, in order to remember that it was the Lord who had made *them* special. The Sabbath set Israel apart from other nations, to keep them from assimilating into the surrounding pagan cultures.

This sabbatical system included three special

times—every week, every seventh year, and every fiftieth year:

- The weekly Sabbath was one day in seven for God's people to rest (Exodus 23:12).

- The annual Sabbath was one year in seven, during which the land was to rest from being worked, for the benefit of the soil and for the poor (Exodus 23:10–11).

- The Jubilee Sabbath was the climax of the sabbatical system, in which freedom was proclaimed throughout Israel every fiftieth year. During the year of Jubilee, debts were cancelled, prisoners and slaves were freed, and alienated land was returned to its former owner (Leviticus 25:8–55).

Sabbath Day Instructions

The Sabbath commandment encompasses both inactivity and proper activity.

- *Keep this day holy.* This day of rest and worship was to be set apart from business as usual. Work was reserved for the rest of the week, but this day was to be set apart totally for God (Exodus 20:8).

- *Work for six days.* Apart from the Sabbath, work was to be done on all other days (Exodus 20:9).

- *Meet for a sacred gathering* (Leviticus 23:3). This was an assembly (convocation) for personal renewal and worshipping God, which Jesus practiced. Psalm 92—titled "A Song for the Sabbath Day"—was commonly used on this occasion.

Specific instructions were given about prohibited work.

- No work was to be done by man or animal (Exodus 20:10).

- No food was to be gathered or prepared (Exodus 16:27–30).

- No fires were to be kindled (Exodus 35:3).

- No fuel was to be gathered for a fire. Numbers 15:32–36 records an incident in which a defiant violator of this law was put death.

- No buying or selling was to occur (Nehemiah 13:15–21).

Reasons for Observing the Sabbath

This is the longest commandment in the Decalogue, and it comes with two supporting reasons for why it should be obeyed: God's rest after creation of the universe, and God's redemption of Israel.

- God's rest after creation of the universe (Exodus 20:11). God created the universe in six days. He then blessed the seventh day and rested (Genesis 1:1–2:3). Omnipotent God didn't rest because He was tired; rather He rested to establish a cycle of six days of work and one day of rest. By honoring the Sabbath, the people declared their belief in God as the Creator.

- God's redemption of Israel (Deuteronomy 5:15). Before the people entered the Promised Land, Moses reviewed the law of God with the younger generation that had survived the forty-year wilderness wanderings (Deuteronomy 5:1–5). He called them to remember that God had liberated the nation from slavery in Egypt, where there had been no regular rest. Observing the Sabbath testified to the people's belief in God as their Redeemer.

A Picture for All to See

Just like the rainbow was a sign
of God's covenant with Noah
(Genesis 9:13), and the ritual of
circumcision was a sign of God's
covenant with Abraham (Genesis
17:11), the Sabbath was a sign of
God's covenant with Israel (Exodus
31:13).

Jesus and the Sabbath

Jesus Himself observed the Sabbath, though He resisted some of the man-made rules that developed over time.

- He regularly kept the Sabbath. Throughout His life, Jesus regularly observed the Sabbath. "And as His custom was, He went into the synagogue on the Sabbath day" (Luke 4:16, emphasis added). After working daily as a carpenter, Jesus rested on the Sabbath and faithfully attended the synagogue.

- He was accused of breaking the Sabbath. On two occasions recorded in Matthew 12, Jesus was accused of breaking the Sabbath. Instead, what he had violated was one of the countless man-made laws developed by the rabbis supposedly to protect the Sabbath. Their thirty-nine categories of forbidden acts had turned the day of rest into a day of rigor. Jesus rejected the commandments of men, and thus He and His disciples were first accused of violating the Sabbath by harvesting grain for personal consumption.

On the second occasion, Jesus healed a man's paralyzed hand. In response to the Pharisees' accusations, Jesus, as the Lord of the Sabbath, clarified the law by explaining what was permissible on the Sabbath:

➤ Acts of necessity (Matthew 12:3–4)
➤ Acts of service to God (Matthew 12:5–6)
➤ Acts of mercy (Matthew 12:7–8)
➤ Acts of kindness (Matthew 12:9–13)

Elsewhere, Jesus summarized a proper perspective on the Sabbath when he said, "The Sabbath was made for man, and not man for the Sabbath" (Mark 2:27).

• He embodied the truth behind the shadow of the law. The book of Hebrews says that the law contained "a shadow of the good things to come" (Hebrews 10:1). Just as the Old Testament sacrifices, temple objects, saints, and sacred days all anticipated various truths about the coming Messiah, so too the Sabbath day of rest contained a picture of the spiritual rest available through salvation in Christ (Colossians 2:16–17). Jesus said, "Come unto Me, all you who labor and are heavy laden, and I will give you rest. Take My yoke upon you and learn from Me, for I am gentle and lowly in heart, and you will find rest for your souls" (Matthew 11:28–29).

Don't Miss the Rest That God Provides!

The Bible presents various aspects of God's rest:

- Physical rest on the Sabbath day (Exodus 20:8–11)

- Spiritual rest of salvation (Matthew 11:28–30)

- Eternal rest in heaven (Revelation 14:13)

On the other hand, there is no rest for the wicked (Revelation 14:11).

THE FOURTH COMMANDMENT— NOW

Christians have continued the weekly cycle of six days for work and one for worship, but with noticeable changes. The similarities are the result of this commandment being a moral law which doesn't end. The changes, meanwhile, result from the shadowy, ceremonial aspects of the law, which have ended. With Christ's sacrificial death, the ceremonial law came to a conclusion, so that this commandment was not restated in the New Testament. While some Sabbath principles still apply, Christians are not under Sabbath laws.

Sabbath Principles that Have Changed

There are three notable differences in worship observances since the time of the apostles:

- The day of worship was changed. Since the early days of the church, Christians have gathered for worship on the first day of the week (Sunday, the day of the Lord's resurrection) instead of on the seventh day (Saturday, the Jewish Sabbath). (See Acts 20:7; 1 Corinthians 16:1–2). In commemorating the day when Christ rose from the dead and appeared to His disciples (John 20:19), Sunday has been identified as the "the Lord's Day" (Revelation 1:10). As B. B. Warfield observed, "Christ took the Sabbath into the grave with Him and brought the Lord's Day out of the grave with Him on the resurrection morn."

The disciples also gathered to commemorate the day of Pentecost, when the Holy Spirit came and established the church by baptizing believers into the body of Christ (Acts 1:4–5; 2:1–4). Some churches today celebrate the seventh Sunday after Easter as Pentecost Sunday.

The early church fathers also testified to the change of day, as can be found in the Epistle of Barnabas (AD 120) and the writings of Justin Martyr (AD 140) and Clement of Alexandria (AD 194).

- The restriction of activities has changed. Because the Sabbath law connected to the Old Covenant was ended, the limitations on Sabbath activities were also removed— though some believers who maintain a Christian Sabbath still promote a variety of restrictions in order to promote the principle of rest.

- The punishment for violating the commandment has been changed. Along with the end of Israel's theocratic government, capital punishment for Sabbath violations is no longer enforced.

Sabbath Principles That Have Remained

Some aspects, however, have not changed from Old Testament times.

- A regular day of worship is still observed. Christians continue to dedicate one day out of seven as a day for worship. The Puritans called this "the market day of the soul"— that is, a day to "do business" with God.

- The practice of assembling for worship has remained. As believers meet, they are to stir one another to "love and good works" (Hebrews 10:24). Christians are also exhorted to faithfully attend gatherings of God's people and not to forsake the local assembly (Hebrews 10:25).

Though the formal Sabbath requirement is no longer in place, God still calls us away from the hectic pace of the world to relax and focus on His Son as our Creator and Redeemer.

On Thee, at the creation,
the light first had its birth,
On Thee, for our salvation, Christ
rose from depths of earth,
On Thee, our Lord, victorious,
the Spirit sent from heaven,
And thus on Thee, most glorious,
a triple light was given.

CHRISTOPHER WORDSWORTH, "O DAY OF
REST AND GLADNESS" (1862)

Discussion Questions

1. Why was there a shift in the Sabbath observance from the seventh day of the week to the first day?
2. What does the Sabbath day shadow (Hebrews 10:1) represent?
3. What actions did Jesus view as acceptable on the Sabbath?
4. What can we do to make our day of worship more meaningful?

5

THE FIFTH COMMANDMENT: PRAISE FOR PARENTS

"Honor your father and your mother, that your days may be long upon the land which the LORD your God is giving you."

EXODUS 20:12

Becoming a parent is an exciting event. On one occasion, three expectant fathers were in a hospital waiting room while their wives were in the process of delivering babies. A nurse came in and announced to one man that his wife had just given birth to twins. "That's a coincidence," he said, "because I play for the Minnesota Twins!" Later, the nurse returned to announce to the second man that he was the father of triplets. "That's amazing," he said, "because I work for the 3M Company." At that point, the third man slipped off his chair and onto the floor. "Are you ill?" the nurse asked. "No," he replied, "but I work for 7–Up!"

The excitement of parenting continues as children learn to crawl and walk and speak. But there is special satisfaction when children, as they grow, learn to honor and respect their parents.

The first four commandments have a vertical focus that emphasizes our relationship with God. This transitional commandment—the fifth—opens a second section of commandments that have a horizontal focus, emphasizing our relationships with other people, beginning with the family. A child's first relationships are experienced within the family. Before they are aware of God's existence, they experience the love and care of their parents. Likewise, in the home, children learn about their parents' authority and the need to honor them.

Learning to honor their parents affects how children will treat other authority figures—at school, on the job, and in public. The apostle Paul said that believers are to give honor to whom honor is due. If the lesson of the fifth commandment isn't taken to heart in childhood, trouble in adulthood can be expected. As St. Augustine asked, "If anyone fails to honor his parents, is there anyone he will spare?"

Sometimes the parenting is filled by stepparents, foster parents, grandparents, or guardians—and these authority figures are also to be honored.

THE FIFTH COMMANDMENT— THEN

The commandment to honor one's parents was taken very seriously in Israel. To honor meant to respect, to value, to highly esteem, and to treat with dignity in private and public settings. A child who treated his father or mother "with contempt" was to be cursed (Deuteronomy 27:16). The command itself does not elaborate on how to honor one's parents, but general principles can be found throughout the Old Testament.

How to Honor One's Parents

Here are six practical examples of ways children can honor their parents:

- *Be obedient* (Jeremiah 35:8–14). The descendants of Rechab were known for their commitment to their father's lifestyle. Speaking through the prophet Jeremiah, God contrasts their respectful behavior with that of the rebellious nation of Israel. In our day and age, obedience to parents has declined markedly. As the Duke of Windsor once observed, "The thing that impresses me most about America is the way parents obey their children."

- *Be receptive to instruction* (Proverbs 1:8). The fear of the Lord can be seen in a child's receptiveness to instruction from his or her parents as God speaks through them. In Israel, parents were viewed as teachers in the home, and spiritual leaders in the community provided assistance to this parental task (Deuteronomy 6:6–9).

- *Be a righteous person* (Proverbs 23:15–16, 24–25). Godly parents hope and pray that their children will grow up to be righteous and wise people. As the apostle John writes in his third epistle, "I have no greater joy than to hear that my children walk in truth" (3 John 4).

- *Be receptive to correction* (Proverbs 29:15). Dealing with a child's sin is not pleasant, but when a child is receptive to correction and discipline, wisdom can come. Two things are said to produce wisdom: "the rod and rebuke." The rod refers to physical punishment, whereas rebuke refers to verbal correction. This treatment is reflected in the adage, "I was brought up at my mother's knees and across my father's." Children are not to be abused physically or verbally, but they are to be lovingly disciplined and corrected. Without such discipline, the parents will inevitably be brought to shame.

• *Have friends who are a good influence* (Proverbs 28:7). Children tend to imitate the conduct of their friends. Friends who display God-honoring conduct will reinforce a parent's efforts to raise good children. Children who choose good friends will protect their parents from shame.

• *Respect their property* (Proverbs 28:24). Children are to be respectful of their parents' possessions. Family ties are no excuse for taking advantage of one's parents and their property—which the Bible says is akin to robbing them: "Whoever robs his father or his mother, and says, 'It is no transgression,' the same is companion to a destroyer."

Reasons to Honor Parents

Children in Bible times had at least four key reasons to honor their parents.

- *The promise to live long and prosper* (Deuteronomy 5:16). Attached to this commandment was a conditional promise for the nation of Israel. It was not an absolute promise that if they honored and obeyed their parents they would live to be a hundred years old and die wealthy. But, as a general principal, an obedient and honoring lifestyle would contribute to national blessings in the Promised Land.

- *The warning of capital punishment* (Exodus 21:15, 17). Honoring one's parents was a serious matter in Israel. The commandments were unmistakably clear: "He who strikes his father or his mother shall surely be put to death. . . . And he who curses his father or his mother shall surely be put to death."

- *As an expression of holy living* (Leviticus 19:1–3). The people of Israel were told repeatedly that they should be holy because

God is holy. Leviticus reveals that true holiness begins in the home by honoring parents and observing the Sabbath. Likewise today, our relationship with God is reflected in our relationship with our parents.

- *As part of a general respect for old age* (Leviticus 19:32). Standing when an older person entered a room was a way of showing honor. This custom has gradually gone by the wayside, along with respect for the elderly. Elihu was a young man who waited to enter the debate between Job and his three friends out of respect for their age: "I am young in years, and you are very old; therefore I was afraid, and dared not declare my opinion to you. I said, 'Age should speak, and multitude of years should teach wisdom.' But there is a spirit in man, and the breath of the Almighty gives him understanding. Great men are not always wise, nor do the aged always understand justice. Therefore I say, 'Listen to me, I also will declare my opinion.'" (Job 32:6–10).

Hate Your Parents?

Jesus taught some startling things that appear to contradict the fifth commandment.

Among them, He talked about *hating* one's father and mother (Luke 14:26). Every parent is horrified to hear their child announce in a tense moment, "I hate you!" So what did Jesus mean?

His lesson about discipleship emphasized priorities in relationships, and the term *hate*, as Jesus used it, is defined as "to love less by comparison" in a parallel text, Matthew 10:37: "He who loves father or mother more than Me is not worthy of Me."

Christ is to be our first love, and other relationships should not interfere with this. It's an issue of *devotion* rather than *emotion*. Following Christ may create conflict from unbelieving parents, and remaining faithful to Him can seem like hatred to others (Matthew 10:34–36).

Jesus honored His parents and left us a perfect example to follow.

THE FIFTH COMMANDMENT— NOW

As time passes, the relationship between children and parents changes—but honoring parents never goes out of style. A breakdown in honor and respect is a sign of the end times (2 Timothy 3:1–2), but, ideally, in three stages of life parents are to be honored—by both young and adult children.

- *The young family.* In this stage, children are under direct parental care. Christian children must obey their parents' lawful commands, as "in the Lord," and because it will result in personal benefit (Ephesians 6:1–3). Children of church leaders must understand that their conduct reflects on their parents' ministry (1 Timothy 3:2–5, 12).

- *The empty nest.* In time, children leave parents to establish their own families—but the fifth commandment still applies. Children should value their parents' advice, as Moses did (Exodus 18:14–24) and as Solomon advises (Proverbs 23:22). Jacob accepted his parents' marriage counseling to build a God-honoring home (Genesis

28:1–7). When children become parents of their own, it is appropriate to acknowledge their parents' effort in raising them (Proverbs 31:28).

- *The golden years.* Aging parents frequently need special assistance from their children. The European proverb, "One father is better at caring for ten children than ten children are for one father," should not characterize Christians. Adult children have a responsibility to care for their parents when their parents become too old to care for themselves (1 Timothy 5:4). Believers who neglect this responsibility make God's commandment "of no effect" (Matthew 15:6) and are guilty of having "denied the faith and [being] worse than an unbeliever" (1 Timothy 5:8). Jesus rebuked the hypocritical Pharisees for neglecting their parents (Matthew 15:3–6); and at the end of His earthly life, He provided for His mother (John 19:26–27).

O give us homes with godly fathers, mothers,
who always place their hope and trust in Him;
Whose tender patience turmoil never bothers,
whose calm and courage trouble cannot dim;
A home where each finds joy in serving others,
and love still shines tho' days be dark and grim.

BARBARA B. HART,
"A CHRISTIAN HOME" (1965)

Discussion Questions

1. Why is family life important?
2. What reasons does the Bible give for obeying this commandment?
3. How can parents help children obey this commandment?
4. How can adult children honor their parents?

6

THE SIXTH COMMANDMENT:
A MATTER OF LIFE AND DEATH

"Thou shalt not kill."
EXODUS 20:13 KJV

It's said that Billy Graham's wife, Ruth, was once asked if she had ever considered divorce during their long marriage. Her humorous response was, "Divorce? No. Murder? Yes!"

Though we can laugh at such a remark, the sixth commandment addresses a serious issue that's as old as time: murder. This commandment is used to oppose war, capital punishment, and the killing of animals. Others use it to oppose abortion and euthanasia. Some see only a contradiction, because the Bible also speaks of sacrificing animals, executing criminals, and God's judgment of death on those who violate His law. Who's right? The answer lies in further Bible study about the actual meaning of the commandment and how it should be applied.

Preliminary Considerations

The Bible does not leave us to wonder what God actually meant by the sixth commandment.

- *The meaning of the Hebrew word.* In the Old Testament, several Hebrew words are used to describe different forms of killing. The specific word used in the sixth commandment, *ratsach,* refers to unlawfully taking a life. Matthew 19:18 translates the literal meaning: "You shall not *murder.*" Most modern Bible translations use the word *murder* to make it clear that the commandment refers to the unlawful taking of human life.

- *God is sovereign over life and death.* In the wake of his tragic losses, Job recognized God's sovereignty and said, "The LORD gave, and the LORD has taken away; Blessed be the name of the LORD" (Job 1:21). Job acknowledged that his children were a gift from the Author of life, and their lives were in His hand. God Himself says, "Now see that I, even I, am He, and there is no God besides Me; I kill and I make alive; I wound and I heal; nor is there any who can deliver from My hand" (Deuteronomy 32:39).

The apostle Peter reminds Christians that God did not spare the world when He brought the flood in Noah's day (only eight people survived), and that only Lot and his two daughters survived the fiery destruction of Sodom and Gomorrah (2 Peter 2:5–7; Genesis 19:15–26).

- *God explains why some people should be killed.* Long before Israel became a nation and received the law, God gave a universal law to mankind that animals could be killed for food, but people were not to be killed unlawfully. God's reason was that mankind was made in His image, which means we are separated from the animals by our rational, moral, and spiritual capacities. There is a difference between men and monkeys (Genesis 9:3–6). Murder is actually an assault on the image of God, both insulting and dishonoring Him. Thus, human life is sacred, and the just punishment for murder, prescribed by God, is the death penalty.

THE SIXTH COMMANDMENT—
THEN

All ancient societies had laws against murder. The Old Testament reveals God's standard and defines the appropriate punishment—and protections—for different ways in which a life can be taken. Thus, it's clear that *all murder is killing but not all killing is murder* (Numbers 35:1–34).

Unlawful Deaths

Scripture defines three types of unlawful killings:

- *Murder* (Numbers 35:16–21). The violent, deliberate, premeditated taking of another person's life is known as homicide. Before the establishment of law enforcement as we know it, the person responsible for tracking down a murderer and applying the death sentence was called "the avenger of blood." This was most often a relative of the victim.

- *Negligent death.* The precept of loving one's neighbors includes the idea of keeping them safe. In Israel, some people died due to the negligence of others who failed to keep their property safe (Deuteronomy

22:8). Others were killed by animals that weren't properly restrained (Exodus 21:28–29). These negligent owners were held responsible and punished accordingly.

- *Killing the unborn* (Exodus 21:22–25). If a pregnant woman was harmed as a bystander to a fight, and her unborn baby died, the attacker would pay with his life. The unborn baby was viewed as a real person with a right to life and the same legal protection as the mother.

Accidental Death

In some circumstances, people were killed accidentally, with no malicious intent (Numbers 35:10–15). God's law provided for the killers a place of asylum—cities of refuge throughout the Promised Land, where they would be safe from the avenger of blood, at least until the facts of the killing could be determined. After hearing all the evidence, city officials would decide whether a person would be permitted to remain under protection within the boundaries of the city of refuge—until the death of the high priest would set him free (Numbers 35:22–28).

Lawful Deaths

Just as the Bible defined three types of unlawful killing, so it describes three types of lawful deaths.

- *Capital punishment.* God established a legal standard of justice for murder: "You shall give life for life" (Exodus 21:23). The punishment for murder was the death penalty (Exodus 21:12). From God's perspective, when one person was murdered, at least one other person should die as a result. This functioned as a deterrent to murder, and also to personal vengeance. Exodus lists other crimes, in addition to murder, that also warranted the death penalty (Exodus 21:14–17; 22:18–24).

    The New Testament has no precept that would nullify the practice of capital punishment. In fact, Romans 13:1–4 reinforces it as a responsibility of the state. (This is one way to understand how a person can be pro-life and yet still support the death penalty.)

- *Self defense.* Homeowners had the right to use force to protect themselves and their families from harm by a nighttime intruder.

If the intruder was killed, the homeowner
would not be considered guilty. However,
if there was a daytime break-in, lethal force
was not to be used, because it could be
more easily determined that the burglar's
motive was theft and not murder (Exodus
22:2–3).

- *War.* In a sin-cursed world, war is a tragic
  reality (Ecclesiastes 3:8). Life in the
  ancient Near East was a hostile military
  environment, and war was a means of
  keeping evil from escalating. Customarily,
  spring was the season when kings led
  their armies into battle, due to favorable
  weather conditions (2 Samuel 11:1). The
  Lord Himself is known as "a man of war"
  (Exodus 15:3). He taught warriors how
  to fight (Psalm 18:34), gave battle plans
  to generals (Joshua 6:1–5), and provided
  victory to his righteous people (Proverbs
  21:31). At times, Israel's enemies realized
  that to declare war against Israel was to
  declare war against God (Exodus 14:25).
  Ultimately, Jesus Christ, the Prince of
  Peace, will be the one who puts an end to
  all wars (Isaiah 2:4).

Biblical Killers

Where sin abounded,
grace abounded much more.

ROMANS 5:20

Three well-known men of faith were involved in murder, but were forgiven by God and eventually used to protect and promote life.

- *Moses.* His first attempt to deliver Israel ended in failure when he killed an Egyptian and had to flee the country (Exodus 2:11–15). Yet God forgave Moses and eventually used him to lead Israel to the Promised Land.

- *David.* To cover his sin of adultery with Bathsheba, King David arranged to have her husband, Uriah, killed in battle (2 Samuel 11). After David repented, the Lord forgave him and used him to unify Israel, establish Jerusalem as a worship center, and make extensive preparations for the building of the first Jewish temple.

- *Paul.* He was an accomplice to the martyrdom of Steven. This proved to be

continued

continued

a turning point in Paul's life, as Steven's
dying message was used by God to turn
this hostile persecutor of Christians
into a holy preacher of the gospel (Acts
22:19–21).

THE SIXTH COMMANDMENT—
NOW

No one disputes that murder is wrong. The question
is, What constitutes murder? In our day, most
evangelical Christians would take a unified stand
against homicide, suicide, abortion, infanticide, and
euthanasia as contrary to God's law.

Much has been written about the sixth
commandment, to encourage Christians to think
biblically and to let those who have broken the
commandment know that total forgiveness is
available through Jesus Christ.

The Root of the Problem

Most people believe that they have kept the sixth
commandment because they've never murdered
anyone. Jesus corrected this shallow understanding
in His day by looking beyond the act and probing
deeper to the heart attitude behind it. He wanted

the self-righteous to see their sin as God does. Jesus' definition of *murder* included unjust anger, which can result in verbal abuse. Thus, everyone is guilty of "hidden homicide" and is in danger of judgment and hell (Matthew 5:21–22). The apostle John defined murder the same way and used expressions of love and hate as a test of genuine faith in God (1 John 3:14–15).

Promoting Life

The commandment not to murder also has a positive side—the protection and promotion of life—as illustrated in the parable of the Good Samaritan. When the two religious leaders chose not to get involved with the man who had been attacked and left for dead, they broke the sixth commandment by their negligence. The third man, the Samaritan, did what he could to keep the man from dying (Luke 10:25–37).

In the Bible, Christians are repeatedly encouraged to provide something tangible to help meet the needs of others. We're to be helpful to orphans and widows in trouble (James 1:27). We're to do more than fill the minds of the needy with seasoned words; we're also to fill their stomachs with food and cover their bodies with clothes (James 2:15–17). Such generosity preserves life and paves the way for sharing the gospel of eternal life, as Jesus did with Nicodemus, the woman at the well, and countless others who were dead in their sins.

> *Rescue the perishing, care for the dying,*
> *Snatch them in pity from sin and the grave;*
> *Weep o'er the erring one, lift up the fallen,*
> *Tell them of Jesus, the mighty to save.*

FANNY J. CROSBY, "RESCUE THE PERISHING" (1870)

Discussion Questions

1. Why is human life sacred?
2. Does this commandment extend to the lives of animals?
3. How did Jesus define murder?
4. What is the positive side of this commandment?

7

THE SEVENTH COMMANDMENT: HOME IMPROVEMENT

"You shall not commit adultery."

EXODUS 20:14

A child who was learning the Ten Commandments in Sunday school came home one day and asked his father, "What does the Bible mean when it says, 'Thou shalt not commit agriculture?'" His quick-witted father replied, "Son, it means you're not supposed to plow in someone else's field."

The answer illustrates the concern of this commandment to keep matrimony holy by faithfulness to one's spouse. God ordained the institution of marriage to be a union of one man and one woman for a lifetime (Genesis 2:21–24). Marital fidelity is upheld throughout scripture.

"He who finds a wife finds a good thing, and obtains favor from the LORD" (Proverbs 18:22). After thirty-five years of marriage, I can personally testify that this is true. God's will is that the marriage relationship be joyous (Ecclesiastes 9:9).

But what has happened in our day? We can say with the prophet Jeremiah, "The land is full of adulterers" (Jeremiah 23:10). Adultery is the willful violation of one's marriage vows through sexual involvement with another person. Sexual activity outside the boundaries of marriage invites God's judgment (Hebrews 13:4).

Sadly, adultery has spread across our land like a wildfire, destroying everything in its path. Statistics tragically reveal that not much difference exists between Christians and non-Christians when it comes to faithlessfulness in marriage.

THE SEVENTH COMMANDMENT—THEN

Family life was a priority in Israel. The fifth commandment protected the family by calling children to honor their parents. The seventh commandment protected the sanctity of the home by prescribing death for the sin of adultery (Leviticus 20:10; Deuteronomy 22:22). Lessons can be learned from stories of David's defeat, Joseph's victory, and the sinless Son of God's teaching.

Tragedy for David

King David's story is a cautionary tale—if he could fall into sexual sin, so can any of us.

- *The crime.* David is known as a man after God's own heart (1 Samuel 13:14), yet his life included the tragic tale of his adultery with Bathsheba, his neighbor's wife. One lesson to be learned from this story is that "we reap what we sow." David's adultery resulted in a pregnancy, which he tried to cover up by having Uriah, Bathsheba's husband, return home from military duty to sleep with his wife. When this plan failed, David made subtle arrangements to have Uriah killed in battle (2 Samuel 11:2–24). David soon married Bathsheba, but God viewed the situation as evil.

- *The consequences.* Charles Spurgeon said, "God does not permit His children to sin successfully." David learned this lesson the hard way. When the prophet Nathan confronted David about his sin, he also announced that "the sword shall never depart from your house" (2 Samuel 12:10), meaning that David would experience violent trouble

and death in his family because he had
caused such trouble in someone else's home.
Though forgiven by God, David indeed
experienced much trouble, including the
death of four sons, three by the sword. David
may have thought that no harm would come
from his adultery; instead, he paid a high and
painful price.

- *The confession.* The good news in this story
  is that forgiveness is available when there
  is repentance and confession. Psalm 51
  records David's confession to God. In it, he
  acknowledges that his sin was ultimately
  against God. David records how his
  conscience was haunted by the event, and
  he asks that his sin be taken away. David
  begged that God would work in his heart
  to make him the man that God wanted
  him to be.

Triumph for Joseph

While David's story provides a warning, Joseph's offers
encouragement for those tempted by sexual sin.

- *Her advances.* Genesis 39 records the
  story of Joseph and the wife of Potiphar,

Joseph's master, who was secretly making adulterous advances toward him (Genesis 39:7, 10). She was like those with "eyes full of adultery. . .that cannot cease from sin" (2 Peter 2:14).

- *His answer.* Joseph resisted this temptation by first mentioning his integrity in his earthly responsibilities (Genesis 39:8–9). Then he referred to his devotion to God by stating that adultery is "great wickedness" and a "sin against God" (Genesis 39:9). His answer won't be heard on soap operas, but it is a great memory verse that can help believers resist temptation.

- *His action.* When Potiphar's wife grabbed Joseph, he ran! The time for reasoning was over. It was now time to leave, and he did so in a dramatic way (Genesis 39:11–12). Though he was falsely accused and imprisoned, it's interesting to see that this chapter ends as it began, with the promise that "the Lord was with him." Joseph's steadfast refusal to commit adultery resulted in future blessing for him (Genesis 39:2–3, 21–23). Joseph's story is one of spiritual and moral victory.

Teaching from Jesus

In Matthew 5:27–30, Jesus corrects the superficial teaching of His day that limited the sin of adultery to the outward deed. He focused on inward desires, the lustful thoughts that make a person guilty of adultery (Matthew 15:19). The attitude that says, "It's okay to look as long as I don't touch," is wrong (Matthew 5:27–28). His solution of plucking out an eye or cutting off a hand was not intended to be taken literally; rather, it is hyperbolic language to indicate that decisive steps must be taken. The problem is not the eye or the hand, but the mind and heart. When temptation threatens, spiritual surgery is required—because a person's destiny is at stake:

If your right eye causes you to sin,
pluck it out and cast it from you;
for it is more profitable for you that
one of your members perish,
than for your whole body to be cast into hell.
And if your right hand causes you to sin,
cut it off and cast it from you;
for it is more profitable for you that
one of your members perish,
than for your whole body to be cast into hell.

MATTHEW 5:29–30

Can Adultery Be Forgiven?

Jesus provided the answer to an adulterous woman in John 8:11: "Neither do I condemn you; go and sin no more."

God can forgive the sin of adultery through our repentant faith in Christ. He expects that those who are forgiven will also forsake their sinful behavior. The prophet Isaiah verified this: "Let the wicked forsake his way, and the unrighteous man his thoughts; let him return to the LORD, and He will have mercy on him; and to our God, for He will abundantly pardon" (Isaiah 55:7).

But can a victim who has been betrayed by an unfaithful mate also forgive adultery? I value the example of believers I've known who have forgiven their unfaithful mates based on scripture: "And be kind to one another, tenderhearted, forgiving one another, even as God in Christ forgave you" (Ephesians 4:32).

THE SEVENTH
COMMANDMENT—NOW

What can be done to keep the moral epidemic of lust and adultery from reaching our hearts and our homes? In this section, we will consider some practical steps from the New Testament.

Things to Be Terminated

To remain sexually pure and protect one's marriage, some things must simply be avoided.

- *Run from compromising situations.* "Flee sexual immorality" (1 Corinthians 6:18). J. B. Phillips's translation of this verse is quite graphic: "Avoid sexual looseness like the plague!" Running the race of the Christian life includes running from circumstances that can result in sin. In morally dangerous situations, we must immediately remove ourselves from temptation.

- *Avoid bad influences.* At times, we sin because of pressure from others—so we must avoid people who set a bad example or entice us to sin. Paul warned that sin functions like leaven (yeast), which can

contaminate our lives, homes, and churches
if not removed (1 Corinthians 5:6–7).
We must separate ourselves from the evil
influence of unbelievers and even those who
claim to be believers (1 Corinthians 5:9–
11). "Do not be deceived: 'Bad company
corrupts good morals'" (1 Corinthians
15:33 NASB).

- *Stop lustful thinking.* The transforming
  power of the gospel renews every aspect
  of a believer's life, including the thought
  life (Romans 12:2). Adultery begins in the
  mind and must be eradicated there. Growth
  in Christian living includes learning to
  bring "every thought into captivity to the
  obedience of Christ" (2 Corinthians 10:5).
  We must join with Job in saying, "I made a
  covenant with my eyes not to look lustfully
  at a girl" (Job 31:1 NIV).

Things to Be Cultivated

It's not enough to say, "I just won't sin." Human
nature being what it is, we need to replace sinful
desires and practices with positive alternatives.

- *Develop a loving marriage.* Because marriage

represents the relationship between Christ and the church, husbands are to be loving leaders as wives lovingly follow (Ephesians 5:22–33). Expressing marital love includes maintaining an intimate physical relationship (1 Corinthians 7:1–5). Matthew Henry summarized the love that Adam had for Eve: "She was not made out of his head to rule over him, nor out of his feet to be trampled upon by him, but out of his side to be equal with him, under his arm to be protected, and near his heart to be beloved."

- *Learn about sin's destructive nature.*
  Christians are in a dangerous spiritual and moral war; therefore, we must "abstain from fleshly lusts that war against the soul" (1 Peter 2:11). This warning must be heeded: "Whoever commits adultery with a woman lacks understanding; he who does so destroys his own soul" (Proverbs 6:32). Sin will take you further than you ever thought you'd stray and cost you more than you ever thought you'd pay.

- *Grow spiritually.* Spiritual growth involves conforming our will to God's, and includes our sanctification—specifically, being set apart as morally pure (1 Thessalonians 4:3–7). This will be accomplished by obedience to God's Word, which asks and answers the question, "How can a young man cleanse his way? By taking heed according to Your word" (Psalm 119:9). Praying earnestly about temptation is also necessary. Jesus taught His disciples to pray, "Lead us not into temptation, but deliver us from evil" (Matthew 6:13 KJV).

Christ, who is always faithful, said to His bride, the church, "I will never leave you nor forsake you" (Hebrews 13:5). Jesus wants those who are married to be faithful to each other, and to show the world how beautiful marriage can be when He is part of our homes.

> *All to Jesus I surrender,*
> *humbly at His feet I bow;*
> *Worldly pleasures all forsaken,*
> *take me Jesus, take me now.*

I surrender all, I surrender all,
All to Thee, my blessed Savior,
I surrender all.

JUDSON W. VAN DE VENTER,
"I SURRENDER ALL" (1896)

Discussion Questions

1. What lessons can we learn from David's sin with Bathsheba?
2. How did Joseph resist temptation?
3. What did Jesus teach about adultery?
4. How can we protect ourselves against the sin of adultery?

8

THE EIGHTH COMMANDMENT: THE NO-THEFT ZONE

"You shall not steal."
EXODUS 20:15

We've all heard about "no parking zones" and "no fly zones." Ladera Vista Junior High School in Fullerton, California, has solved the problem of stealing at school by declaring the campus a "no-theft zone." Students are prohibited from having cell phones, iPods, and MP3 players on campus, thus eliminating the theft of such items on school property.

The Christian life should be a personal no-theft zone. Refusing to steal is a matter of obedience to God, personal integrity, and love for our neighbors. The eighth commandment protects the sanctity of private property—focusing on how we treat another person's possessions and how we use our own. If this commandment is to have the effect that God desires, we must understand three fundamental truths:

- *God owns everything.* The Lord says, "All the

earth is Mine" (Exodus 19:5). Everything was created by God, and because He made it all, He owns it all. David declared, "The earth is the LORD's, and everything in it, the world, and all who live in it" (Psalm 24:1 NIV). What we possess we call our own—but it really all belongs to God, including our lives.

- *God gives us what we have (and what we need).* In 1 Chronicles 29:12, David praises God, saying, "Both riches and honor come from You, and You reign over all." It's true that our diligence or laziness contributes to how much we own, but God in His sovereignty entrusts to us as stewards that which belongs to Him, so that we can use these possessions to accomplish His will.

- *God holds us accountable for what He has given us.* Paul writes, "Each of us shall give account of himself to God" (Romans 14:12). One day, all believers will describe to God how they've used the abilities, opportunities, and possessions that He provided. Whether we used all we had for selfish purposes or for blessing others and glorifying God, that day will reveal it.

THE EIGHTH COMMANDMENT— THEN

The Old Testament established personal property rights. Because ancient society was largely agricultural, many laws had to do with farming—but there was also wider application. Specific laws relating to theft can be categorized into at least four groups of circumstances.

- *Relationships between individuals.*
  - ➤ People were not to secretly steal, defraud, or aggressively rob others (Leviticus 19:11, 13).
  - ➤ Stone landmarks indicating property boundaries were not to be moved (Deuteronomy 19:14).
  - ➤ Borrowed money or possessions were to be repaid or returned on time (Psalm 37:21).
  - ➤ Loans between believers were not to include interest (Deuteronomy 23:19–20).
  - ➤ Aiding and abetting theft was still viewed as theft (Proverbs 29:24).

- *Acts of kindness and justice.*
  - ➤ When finding something that had been lost by someone else, it was to be returned to its owner. No "finders keepers, losers weepers" (Exodus 23:4).
  - ➤ Unintentional property damage required compensation (Exodus 22:5–6).
  - ➤ Gleaning food on someone else's property by the poor was not viewed as theft; instead, it was a social provision for the hungry. Gleaners were encouraged to eat their fill, but no doggy bags were allowed (Deuteronomy 23:24–25), except during harvest time when gleaners would follow the field workers (Deuteronomy 24:19–22).

- *Commercial situations involving business.*
  - ➤ Merchants were not to rob consumers by intentionally misrepresenting products for sale to increase profits (Proverbs 11:1).
  - ➤ Land owners were not to defraud or rob their day laborers by withholding their pay (Deuteronomy 24:15).

- *Spiritual situations involving God.*
  - "Will a man rob God?" (Malachi 3:8). The startling answer was yes! Israel's sin of disobedience blinded them to the fact that they were guilty of stealing from God. They pleaded innocent to the charge; but from God's perspective, they were guilty of theft by failing to give their tithes and offerings. When people run from God in disobedience, they usually take with them what belongs to Him (Malachi 3:7–10).

Judicial Reaction to Theft

Degrees of just punishment were prescribed based on the circumstances of the theft and the value of the objects stolen. Punishment always included restitution and sometimes execution.

- A person caught in the act of stealing had to pay back double what was taken (Exodus 22:4)

- Stolen sheep that were slaughtered or sold had to be paid back four for one (Exodus 22:1).

- Stolen oxen that were slaughtered or sold had to be paid back five for one. (Exodus 22:1)

- Stolen food had to be repaid sevenfold (Proverbs 6:30–31).

- Execution was the prescribed punishment for kidnapping another person (Exodus 21:16)

- The tragic story of Achan's theft from Jericho ended with his execution:

Then Joshua, and all Israel with him, took Achan the son of Zerah, the silver, the garment, the wedge of gold, his sons, his daughters, his oxen, his donkeys, his sheep, his tent, and all that he had, and they brought them to the Valley of Achor. And Joshua said, "Why have you troubled us? The LORD will trouble you this day." So all Israel stoned him with stones; and they burned them with fire after they had stoned them with stones.

JOSHUA 7:20–25

"Why Do You Steal?"

Here are some of the top excuses that thieves give to trivialize their sin:

- "I thought it would be exciting, and I knew it wouldn't hurt anyone."
- "They have so much. I knew they wouldn't miss it."
- "My employer should be paying me more."
- "The devil made me do it."
- "Everybody does it."

Achan didn't give excuses for his theft, but in his confession he gave a proper assessment: "I saw... I coveted... I took ... I hid" (Joshua 7:20–21).

Jesus Encountered Thieves

Jesus said, "I am the good shepherd"—comparing Himself to Israel's spiritual leaders, who were bad shepherds without divine authority. Jesus called them "thieves and robbers" (John 10:8). Their false teaching robbed people of God's truth and blessing, whereas Jesus had been appointed by His Father to teach truth and give His life to provide abundant life for His sheep (John 10:1–18).

On three other occasions, Jesus confronted theft:

- *Cleansing of the temple.* In this story, Jesus deals with theft by *judging it.* People traveling a great distance to worship at the Jerusalem temple could buy sacrificial animals and exchange foreign currency on location. The problem was that people were overcharged, making the transactions a legalized theft in the name of God. Jesus single-handedly took action to cleanse the "house of prayer" that had become a "den of thieves" (Matthew 21:12–13).

- *Conversion of a tax collector.* In this story, Jesus eliminates theft by *forgiving it.* Overcharging citizens who owed taxes was practiced by Jewish tax collectors and sanctioned by the Roman Empire, making tax collection a legalized theft in the name of the government. Zacchaeus, who was guilty of this sin, experienced transforming change when he was saved during his encounter with Jesus. His new life produced generosity to the poor, including personal downsizing and self-imposed restitution to victims of his evil methods (Luke 19:1–10).

- *Crucifixion with thieves.* In this story, Jesus removes theft by *bearing it.* Being executed between two thieves added to His humiliation, because the impression was given that He too was a criminal. But this scene fulfilled Bible prophecy about His association with sinners—dying as their sinless substitute and bearing the punishment for their sin. He was the friend of sinners in life and in death (Mark 15:25–28). An immediate result of His sacrifice was the salvation of one of the dying thieves (Luke 23:39–43).

THE EIGHTH COMMANDMENT— NOW

A university survey of 323 teenagers revealed that more than 90 percent thought that theft was wrong, but they weren't sure why. The most common reason given was that they might get caught. But this is simply an issue of love for God and our neighbor. The commandment is restated in the New Testament with comprehensive instruction for Christians in Ephesians 4:28.

Don't Steal

Theft characterizes the lost. Christians who practice theft are to turn away from this conduct, because it represents how unbelievers act (1 Corinthians 6:9–10).

Theft in the twenty-first century may vary from that in Bible times, but it's still theft. The following list reveals new methods of stealing. People may not recognize the theft, but God knows.

- *Time theft.* This is stealing work time that should be given to one's employer. Examples of time theft include making personal phone calls at work, surfing the Internet, taking fake sick days, and spending too much time at the water cooler.

Christians are to make the gospel attractive by their good work ethic (Titus 2:9–10).

- *Identity theft.* Someone's identity is now stolen every three seconds in our society.

- *Literary theft.* Plagiarism is stealing someone else's words and taking credit for them as your own.

- *Music theft.* A copyright produces private property that can be sold. Music theft, or piracy, is copying or downloading music from the Internet without paying for it. Receiving stolen property is also theft!

- *Credit theft.* This is the abuse of credit cards to live beyond our means without being able to pay our bills. God provides for our *needs*, but we provide for our *greeds*.

Do Honest Work

Christians are not to steal to acquire wealth, but to work for it. *Work* is a four letter word, but it's not a bad thing. Paul spoke of the example he set of working to provide for himself and others (Acts 18:3; 20:33–35; 2 Thessalonians 3:7–9), and he warned those who refused to work (2 Thessalonians 3:6–12).

Donate to the Poor

Three points from John Wesley's sermon on Luke 16:9, titled "The Use of Wealth," are appropriate:

- Gain all you can

- Save all you can

- Give all you can.

We won't have to look far to find someone who could use our help. We can put money in an envelope to help others, but it will be a greater blessing to put it into their hands. "It is more blessed to give than to receive" (Acts 20:35).

> *Take my lips and let them be*
> *Filled with messages from Thee;*
> *Take my silver and my gold,*
> *Not a mite would I withhold.*

FRANCES R. HAVERGAL,
    "TAKE MY LIFE AND LET IT BE" (1874)

Discussion Questions

1. Why has God entrusted us with our possessions?
2. What reasons can we give for not stealing?
3. Do we have any borrowed items that need to be returned?
4. What are ways that theft is committed without our realizing it?

9

THE NINTH COMMANDMENT: LANGUAGE MANAGEMENT

"You shall not bear false witness against your neighbor."
EXODUS 20:16

A person prayed, "Lord, so far today, I've done all right. I haven't gossiped or lost my temper. I haven't been grumpy, greedy, or overindulgent, and I'm thankful for that. In a few moments, I'm going to get out of bed and then I'll probably need a lot more help. Amen."

This comical prayer illustrates the power of sin in people's lives. This problem starts early when cute little babies learning to talk start lying (Psalm 58:3).

God has established the standard for acceptable speech: "Let there be no more foul language, but good words instead—words suitable for the occasion, which God can use to help other people" (Ephesians 4:29 PHILLIPS). Some evil conversation is painfully obvious; other is more subtle, such as gossip, slander, and what's trivially called "little white lies." Some people seem to approve of these sins by their involvement in them, but Jesus said, "Those things which proceed out of the mouth come from the heart, and they defile a man" (Matthew 15:18).

William Hendriksen stated the concern correctly: "In our own day. . .many warnings are being issued against air pollution and water pollution. Christ's implied warning against the incalculably more ominous evil of mouth pollution and heart pollution is certainly needed." Rotten words reveal a spiritual heart problem that only Christ can solve (Romans 3:10–14, 21–22).

The ninth commandment is about controlling what we say about others. To love our neighbor is to speak good to them and about them. The third commandment protects God's name; the ninth commandment protects our name and our neighbor's name.

Words can be helpful or harmful. "Death and life are in the power of the tongue" (Proverbs 18:21), and "Reckless words pierce like a sword, but the tongue of the wise brings healing" (Proverbs 12:18 NIV). In the Disney movie *Bambi*, Thumper says, "If you can't say anything nice, don't say nothin' at all." We've been taught that "sticks and stones can break my bones but words will never hurt me." Well, guess what? Words *do* hurt! So we should concentrate on managing our language.

THE NINTH COMMANDMENT— THEN

The God of truth made clear His attitude toward sinful speech. Included in a list of things that He hates are "a lying tongue...a false witness who speaks lies" (Proverbs 6:17, 19). God's words are always honest and dependable. "God is not a man that He should lie.... Has He spoken, and will He not make it good?" (Numbers 23:19). Just as parents teach their children to talk, so too does God instruct His children in how to speak properly. "A righteous man hates lying" (Proverbs 13:5).

The Courtroom Setting

The ninth commandment places us in a courtroom setting where witnesses must speak the truth if justice is to prevail. Customarily, a witness is asked to answer the following oath: "Do you solemnly swear to tell the truth, the whole truth, and nothing but the truth, so help you God?" By contrast, in ancient Israel's legal system, a number of divine guidelines were followed to secure the truth from witnesses.

- *A plurality of witnesses.* Two or three corroborating witnesses were required to establish the guilt of a person accused of a crime (Deuteronomy 19:15).

- *A perjury penalty.* As a powerful deterrent to lying to the court, those giving false testimony would be sentenced to the same punishment that would have been imposed on the accused, including execution (Deuteronomy 19:16–19). "Those who remain shall hear and fear, and hereafter they shall not again commit such evil among you. Your eye shall not pity: life shall be for life, eye for eye, tooth for tooth, hand for hand, foot for foot" (Deuteronomy 19:20–21).

- *A participant in execution.* It's one thing to accuse someone of a crime, but it's quite another thing to be required to initiate the execution of the accused upon conviction. But such was the requirement in ancient Israel. "The hands of the witnesses shall be the first against him to put him to death" (Deuteronomy 17:7).

- *A proclamation requirement.* A witness who withheld valuable evidence that could influence a case would be guilty of sin. Witnesses were required to volunteer their testimony (Leviticus 5:1).

The Casual Setting

The ninth commandment also applies to daily conversations. There may be more concern in a courtroom to choose words carefully, because every word is scrutinized, but it's also important to remember that God knows every word we speak (Psalm 139:4) and holds us accountable for what we say (Matthew 12:36). The commandment against bearing false witness can be violated in several ways:

- *Lying.* Speaking false words about another person with an intention to deceive through fabrication, exaggeration, perversion, omission, or addition to the truth is a sin (Exodus 23:1–2). To lie is to imitate the devil, the father of lies (John 8:44).

- *Gossip.* Gossip is anything said about another person that should not be spoken. What's said may be true or only a rumor, but it has the potential to harm the other person's reputation (Proverbs 18:8). A gossip is also called a "whisperer," who ruins friendships (Proverbs 16:28), and a "talebearer," who can't be trusted (Proverbs 11:13). Gossip should never be packaged as "a prayer request" to spread to other people!

- *Slander.* Slander is speaking damaging words with an intention to harm someone. God calls this "giving your mouth to evil" as you "speak against" someone, even those very close to you (Psalm 50:19–20). It is also known as backbiting (Psalm 15:3).

The Counseling Session

Throughout the Old Testament, instructions are found for correcting disobedience and encouraging obedience to this commandment. The following scriptures should govern our words.

- *Pray for help.* "Set a guard, O LORD, over my mouth; keep watch over the door of my lips" (Psalm 141:3). Many athletes use a mouth guard to protect their teeth. Psalm 141 is a request for a mouth guard to sanctify our words. One of my Christian friends was so serious about "setting a guard" over her mouth that she kept this verse displayed near her phone. People use mouthwash for clean breath and toothpaste for clean teeth—but for clean words, prayer is needed.

- *Maintain fellowship with God.* "Can two walk together, unless they are agreed?" (Amos 3:3). Experiencing communion with God requires that believers practice holiness, including in the words that they speak about other people (Psalm 15:1–3).

- *Be determined to obey.* The psalmist says, "I will guard my ways, lest I sin with my tongue; I will restrain my mouth with a muzzle, while the wicked are before me" (Psalm 39:1). Some people have been hurt by untamed animals; others by an untamed tongue.

- *Discourage evil speaking.* We should not be the kind of people who have our ears tuned to evil conversations about other people. The apostle Paul spoke strongly against those who "approve of those who practice" sin—including whispering and backbiting (Romans 1:28–32).

- *Commit yourself to God.* Jesus patiently endured many untrue and hurtful words spoken about Him, but He entrusted each situation to His Father. "Commit your way the LORD, trust also in Him, and He shall bring it to pass" (Psalm 37:5). The Lord's tolerant reaction to mistreatment during His trials is an amazing example for every Christian. His secret was that He "committed Himself to Him who judges righteously" (1 Peter 2:23). Jesus always spoke the right words at the right time in the right way for the right reasons—and so should we.

So all bore witness to Him,
and marveled at the gracious words
which proceeded out of His mouth.
And they said, "Is this not Joseph's son?"

LUKE 4:22

T-H-I-N-K

Alan Redpath, former pastor at Moody Memorial Church in Chicago (1953–1962), recommended that we give ourselves a "think before you speak" test by asking ourselves five questions:

T: "Is it *T*rue?"
H: "Is it *H*elpful?"
I: "Is it *I*nspiring?"
N: "Is it *N*ecessary?"
K: "Is it *K*ind?"

If what we're about to say doesn't pass this test, it's best to keep quiet.

The heart of the righteous studies how to answer, but the mouth of the wicked pours forth evil.
PROVERBS 15:28

THE NINTH COMMANDMENT— NOW

Foreigners are easily identified by their speech, which sounds very different from a native speaker's. This is how it should be for Christians, whose speech is not to conform to the ways of the world. Two scripture texts provide guidance for how Christians should talk. The first deals with the human inability to control our tongues (that is, our words), and the second focuses on how our conversations can be changed to please God and honor our neighbors.

Taming Our Tongue

The epistle of James addresses the futility of trying to control the tongue by mere human effort. "No man can tame the tongue. It is an unruly evil, full of deadly poison. . . . Out of the same mouth proceed blessing and cursing" (James 3:8, 10). The tongue must be bridled, like a horse, and held under steady control, like the rudder of a ship, to keep us from defiling ourselves through a lack of self-control. It is only through "wisdom from above"—which "is first pure, then peaceable, gentle, willing to yield, full of mercy and good fruits, without partiality and without hypocrisy" (James 3:17)—that we can tame the tongue and manage how we speak.

Transforming Our Talk

The letter to the Ephesians reveals that a Christian's "worthy walk" includes worthy talk—"speaking the truth in love" (Ephesians 4:15). Lying is to be replaced by truthfulness between believers, because it strengthens our unity in Christ (Ephesians 4:25). Corrupt words that tear down are to be replaced by choice words that build up and provide a blessing to the hearer (Ephesians 4:29). Angry, loud, slanderous words are to be replaced by tenderhearted words of forgiveness (Ephesians 4:31–32).

Believers must resist the devil, who persistently tries to gain a foothold in our lives and contaminate our talk (Ephesians 4:27). And we must remember that we are not to grieve the Holy Spirit, who has done so much for us (Ephesians 4:30).

According to some estimates, the average person speaks enough words in a typical week to fill a five hundred page book! We might be disappointed to read some of the things we said last week. Let's remember that, as God's children, we are His witnesses to our neighbors (Acts 1:8), and we must speak to them words of eternal life.

Perhaps today there are loving
words which Jesus would have me speak;
There may be now, in the paths of sin, some
wanderer whom I should seek.
O Savior, if Thou wilt be my Guide,
tho' dark and rugged the way,
My voice shall echo the message sweet,
I'll say what you want me to say.

MARY H. BROWN, "I'LL GO WHERE YOU
WANT ME TO GO" (1894)

Discussion Questions

1. Can you explain the acronym T-H-I-N-K?
2. How is the devil involved when we sin with our mouths?
3. What practical steps can we take to have victory in our conversations?
4. What are some biblical prayers about our speech?

9

THE TENTH COMMANDMENT: CONTENTMENT 101

"You shall not covet."

EXODUS 20:17

The story is told of a time when President Abraham Lincoln was carrying his two crying sons. When someone asked what was wrong with the boys, Lincoln replied, "Exactly what's wrong with the whole world. . . . I have three walnuts and each boy wants two."

This story reflects the essence of the tenth commandment: the sin of covetousness and the virtue of contentment. The word *covet* means "to have an intense desire." It is used in the Bible in both a positive and negative way. The apostle Paul encourages believers to "covet to prophesy" (1 Corinthians 14:39 KJV). When someone says, "I covet your prayers" they're expressing a legitimate desire for something good. But sin has spread so deeply into our desires that we must beware of private, evil desires, such as coveting other people's possessions (Proverbs 21:10).

This commandment differs from the others in that it goes beyond our outward behavior and probes at the level of our internal attitudes where sin begins. It reveals that God looks at our hearts, and He desires integrity, honesty, and sincerity (1 Samuel 16:7; Psalm 51:6).

The Westminster Shorter Catechism puts it like this: "The tenth commandment forbiddeth all discontentment with our own estate, envying or grieving at the good of our neighbor, and all inordinate motions and affections to anything that is his." The Bible describes covetousness as "foolish and harmful lusts which drown men in destruction and perdition" (1 Timothy 6:9). Paul says that such people will be excluded from heaven (1 Corinthians 6:9–10). It is because of this sin that the fallen angels lost heaven, Adam and Eve lost Eden, and the people of Judah lost their nation. Covetous people will never be satisfied, as there is always more to be desired— and riches never satisfy (Ecclesiastes 5:10–11).

This serious sin is largely ignored by most people. You'll never see a headline that says, MAN FOUND GUILTY OF COVETOUSNESS. No, in our society, the desire for more is applauded. In fact, covetousness is the driving force behind much of the advertising we see. But like termites in the walls, covetousness produces unseen damage in our lives. We can be sure that it's a serious sin in God's eyes, which is why He included it in the Decalogue. The question is, How serious is it to us?

THE TENTH COMMANDMENT— THEN

Listed in the commandment are a number of our neighbor's possessions that we are not to covet: our neighbor's house, our neighbor's spouse, our neighbor's servants, and our neighbor's animals. In an agricultural society where wealth was measured by the size of one's herds and one's household, these specific prohibitions were relevant. For our purposes, though, the final prohibition sums it all up: "You shall not covet. . .anything that is your neighbor's" (Exodus 20:17).

Let's look at three Old Testament incidents where coveting caused calamities.

Achan Was Achin'

After Israel's miraculous victory at Jericho, the people experienced a stunning defeat at Ai because of a hidden sin—covetous theft by a Jewish soldier. God revealed that Achan was the culprit; and though his public confession, "I have sinned," sounded spiritual, it was offered only after he had been found out.

Because he didn't deal with his covetousness, it grew into disobedience, deception, and disaster. When it was over, thirty-six fellow soldiers had died, and Achan and his family, who had conspired with him, were executed. He buried what he stole, and then Israel buried him. Achan was achin' because of his sin (Joshua 7:1–26).

Ahab Was Annoyed

King Ahab owned two palaces and plenty of land. What more could he want? Yet he coveted Naboth's vineyard. Ahab made a generous offer to acquire the land, but Naboth refused, in order to obey God and keep the property in his family (1 Kings 21:1–3; Leviticus 25:23–28).

Ahab's childish reaction was to fall on his bed, bury his face in his pillow, and refuse to eat! His evil wife, Jezebel, used the local court system to have Naboth and his sons murdered, so that she could seize the land to give to Ahab (1 Kings 21:4–16). But covetousness had a boomerang effect, resulting in the deaths of both Ahab and Jezebel. "So are the ways of everyone who is greedy for gain; it takes away the life of its owners" (Proverbs 1:19).

Jesus Was Admonishing

To those who spend their energy trying to secure earthly wealth while neglecting their spiritual needs, Jesus asks some searching questions: "For what profit is it to a man if he gains the whole world, and loses his own soul? Or what will a man give in exchange for his soul?" (Matthew 16:26). When we ask how much a person is worth, we really mean, How much do they own? Our eternal soul is worth more than all of earth's wealth.

To relatives squabbling over an inheritance, Jesus warned, "Take heed and beware of covetousness, for one's life does not consist in the abundance of the things he possesses" (Luke 12:15). He then taught a parable about a successful but foolish man, emphasizing the point that all wealth is left behind at death, and that death is imminent.

"I will say to my soul,
'Soul, you have many goods laid up for many years;
take your ease; eat, drink, and be merry.'
But God said to him, 'Fool!
This night your soul will be required of you;
then whose will those things be which you have provided?'
So is he who lays up treasure for himself,
and is not rich toward God."

LUKE 12:19–21

Am I Covetous?

It can be hard to tell, but here are some symptoms:

- Experiencing a gnawing anxiety for what we don't have

- Ungrateful complaining because we don't have what other people have

- Abusing the use of credit cards in spite of growing financial debt

- Hoarding what we own and not being generous

- Feeling we could harm someone to get what we want

THE TENTH COMMANDMENT—
NOW

Covetousness permeates our society like the invisible air we breathe. Feeding our contemporary problem of materialism and consumerism are ads telling us that happiness is just a purchase away. And oh, by the way, you're worth it and you deserve it!

When desires are driven by sin, people take matters into their own hands, fighting to get what they want, rather than trusting God to supply their needs. Some who do pray don't have their prayers answered because they pray with selfish motives, wanting their own will to be done rather than seeking God's will (James 4:1–3; 1 John 5:14).

God reveals that many false teachers are driven by covetousness, viewing religion as an opportunity to get rich (2 Peter 2:1–3, 14); and this problem will increase in the last days (2 Timothy 3:1–2). These charlatans stand in contrast to true ministers of God, who are not to be motivated by money (1 Timothy 3:2–3).

Before the apostle Paul became a believer, he promoted the popular but false message that acceptance from God comes by doing our best to keep His commandments. Then God showed him that his best efforts were unacceptable, and that he was a guilty sinner like everyone else. Paul's subsequent testimony revealed that God used the commandment about covetousness to humble him, so that he cried out like the repentant tax collector, "God, be merciful to me a sinner" (Romans 7:7–11; Luke 18:13).

Learning Contentment

As Paul placed his faith in Jesus Christ, his life was dramatically changed. He learned to replace covetousness with contentment. His life and ministry were not covered by "a cloke of covetousness" (1 Thessalonians 2:5 KJV). Here are three things Paul discovered that can also help us.

- *A perspective on prosperity.* Some people's ultimate priority seems to be accumulating earthly wealth to gain "the good life." But Paul learned that "godliness with contentment is great gain" (1 Timothy 6:6). True wealth comes from being satisfied with God's provisions for this life and knowing the Lord, which prepares us for eternity. This is, by far, the good life! We must remember that everyone exits this life the same way they entered it—with nothing. When anyone asks how much a deceased person left behind, the answer is always the same. . . everything (1 Timothy 6:7; Job 1:21).

- *The promise of God.* People who have a hard time finding contentment are looking in the wrong places. They can discover it by trusting God's promises in scripture. One such promise related to contentment is found in Hebrews 13:5: "I will never leave you nor forsake you." The point is that God will always be present to help us in our deepest need or most desperate circumstance. Our contentment will be as solid as our trust in the promises of God.

- *The power of Christ.* In his letter to the Philippians, Paul says that he has learned the secret of being content in spite of outward circumstances of poverty or prosperity: He has learned to depend on God. "I can do all things through Christ who strengthens me" (Philippians 4:13) Earlier in the same letter, he says, "It is God who works in you both to will and to do for His good pleasure" (Philippians 2:13), which echoes what Jesus taught: "Without

Me you can do nothing" (John 15:5). This reliance on the power of God was the secret that Paul wanted everyone to learn. As the psalmist prayed, "Incline my heart to Your testimonies, and not to covetousness" (Psalm 119:36).

When you look at others with
*   their lands and gold,*
Think that Christ has promised you
*   His wealth untold;*
Count your many blessings. Money cannot buy
Your reward in heaven, nor your
*   home on high.*

JOHNSON OATMAN JR., "COUNT YOUR
     BLESSINGS" (1897)

Discussion Questions

1. Why is covetousness such an ignored sin?
2. What was Jesus talking about when He referred to giving something in exchange for your soul?
3. What does covetousness cause people to forget?
4. How can we defeat this sin when it's present in us?

Epilogue: Searching for Life

"Good Teacher, what good thing shall
I do that I may have eternal life?"
Matthew 19:16

The National Radio Astronomy Observatory in the Allegheny Mountains of West Virginia is a fascinating facility that scans deep into outer space using the world's largest fully steerable radio telescope. During a question and answer session for visitors, I asked about the major purposes for maintaining the facility. The answer was that, in addition to discovering the unknown mysteries of the universe, they have the ability to know if alien intelligence tries to approach or contact Earth. Among other things, they search for extraterrestrial life.

During tragic disasters, when buildings collapse and victims are trapped under rubble, there is a short window of time when rescue workers can try to recover survivors, sometimes using trained search dogs. They search for physical life.

The New Testament describes an encounter between Jesus and a rich, young ruler who was searching for another kind of life—spiritual life. Most Christians would not think of doing what Jesus did. He directed the conversation to a discussion about the Ten Commandments (Matthew 19:16–22; Mark 10:17–22; Luke 18:18–23).

Like most people, this man felt a spiritual need and wondered what would happen to him when he died. In spite of his wealth and accomplishments, he still wanted what money can't buy and earthly accomplishments can't provide: eternal life.

So he approached the One whom he believed had the answers. Peter had come to the same conclusion about Jesus, saying to Him, "You have the words of eternal life" (John 6:68). And Jesus said of Himself, "I give them eternal life, and they shall never perish" (John 10:28). To make the same point, Ravi Zacharias said, "Jesus did not come to make bad people good, but to make dead people live!"

Let's consider the role of the Ten Commandments in Jesus' response to the rich young ruler.

A Personal Question

There were three elements to Jesus' interaction with this wealthy seeker.

- *The inquiry.* The rich man's hunger for life motivated him to run to Jesus and publicly kneel in front of Him to ask his burning question about eternal life (Mark 10:17). He's ready to be saved. . .or is he?

Jesus first tried to correct the flawed opinions the man had of himself and of Jesus. He questioned him about his use of the title "Good Teacher," saying, "Why do you call Me good? No one is good but One, that is, God" (Mark 10:18). Far from denying His own deity, Jesus was revealing that this man needed a higher view of Jesus—as God, who alone is inherently good and thus should be obeyed.

The man also needed a lower opinion of himself. Although he was uncertain about his place in heaven, he still viewed himself as a nice guy, who wasn't really that bad (Mark 10:19–20). He needed to see himself as God saw him—as a sinner (Romans 3:10–18, 23).

The man then asked the question of all questions: "What good thing shall I do that I may have eternal life?" (Matthew 19:16). Because he had been raised in a religious system that erroneously taught that righteousness was earned by doing moral and religious works, he simply wanted to make sure he had already done enough.

- *The instructions.* Because salvation has always been by grace through faith, what Jesus said to the rich, young ruler might be surprising: "If you want to enter into life, keep the commandments" (Matthew 19:17). Jesus wasn't teaching salvation by works—he was simply meeting the man at his own level of understanding about the law. Warren Wiersbe said, "Jesus did not introduce the law to show the man how to be saved, but to show him that he needed to be saved." As the apostle Paul learned by experience, "by the law is the knowledge of sin" (Romans 3:20). According to Deuteronomy 27:26, a curse was imposed on everyone who did not obey the law perfectly. And James says, "Whoever shall keep the whole law, and yet stumble in one point, he is guilty of all" (James 2:10).

  As Jesus quoted the last half of the Ten Commandments, the tenth commandment was conspicuous by its absence—suggesting that it was the man's main problem, of which he was still unaware (Matthew 19:18–19).

- *The invitation.* Like a doctor prodding a patient's body in order to locate a problem,

Jesus diagnosed the man's heart and found he was covetous, loving money more than he loved God. Jesus told the man to do three things to gain "treasure in heaven": sell his earthly treasure, give to the poor, and follow Jesus (Matthew 19:21). Again, Jesus was not establishing universal requirements for salvation; he was dealing with an individual to expose his sin and lead him to a saving faith.

The man was now forced to consider his sin—and he ultimately rejected the Savior's offer. He got up from his knees and walked away in sadness (Matthew 19:22).

A Theological Question

After the man had gone, Jesus used the encounter as a teachable moment for His disciples, quoting a proverb to make his point: "It is easier for a camel to go through the eye of a needle than for a rich man to enter the kingdom of God" (Matthew 19:24).

Because it was customary for the Jews of that day to view wealth as a sign of God's favor, and poverty as a sign of punishment for sin, it was hard for them to imagine how anyone could be saved. The disciples, absolutely stunned by what Jesus said, asked the obvious theological question: "Who then can be saved?" (Luke 18:26).

Jesus responded, "With men this is impossible, but with God all things are possible" (Matthew 19:26). His response echoes a conversation centuries before, when God asked Abraham a rhetorical question: "Is anything too hard for the LORD?" (Genesis 18:14). The answer, of course, was no. God saves people who we can't imagine could be saved. Here are two examples:

- *Zacchaeus was saved.* To illustrate the power of God's saving grace, Luke 19:1–10 describes the salvation of an unlikely rich tax collector named Zacchaeus. When he met Jesus he "received Him joyfully" into his home and his heart (Luke 19:6). As a result, Zacchaeus's life was transformed, such that he became extremely generous and followed divine principals of restitution to anyone who had experienced loss from his heavy-handed tax collecting methods (Luke 19:8).

- *Paul was saved.* Another wealthy person who was saved was the Pharisee Saul of Tarsus, later renamed Paul. For many believers at the time, this news seemed impossible because of Paul's previous persecution of Christians (Acts 9:26). Though accepted by God, Paul viewed himself as the worst of sinners because of his former hostilities against the church. He said, "Christ Jesus came into the world to save sinners, of whom I am chief" (1 Timothy 1:15).

A Final Question

Having arrived at the end of this study of the Ten Commandments, a final question is in order: Have you received God's gift of eternal life through Jesus Christ our Lord?

God still offers life today. It's one thing to read about a young man who rejected the opportunity to receive eternal life and of others who did take it—but all study of scripture must ultimately lead us to ask, "How does this apply to me?"

The Bible is clear that God's law was designed to expose our sin and produce our confession: "I have sinned." Scripture then guides us to the Savior, who gives pardon and life.

Let's consider a passage that combines thoughts about the Ten Commandments and Christ: "He has

. . .forgiven you all trespasses, having wiped out the handwriting of requirements that was against us, which was contrary to us. And He has taken it out of the way, having nailed it to the cross" (Colossians 2:13–14).

Frequently, those being crucified had a list of their crimes nailed to their cross. The law we all broke was metaphorically nailed to the cross with Jesus, and by His death He paid our debt in full by suffering the curse of the law.

F. F. Bruce said, "He took that signed confession of indebtedness, which stood as a perpetual witness against you, and cancelled it in His death."

This is what can be called real debt-free living! Those who have been set free by God's Son can say, "This is love for God: to obey his commands. And his commands are not burdensome" (1 John 5:3 NIV).

> *By God's Word at last my sin I learned,*
> *Then I trembled at the law I'd spurned,*
> *Till my guilty soul imploring turned to*
> *Calvary.*
> *Mercy there was great and grace was free,*
> *Pardon there was multiplied to me,*
> *There my burdened soul found liberty at*
> *Calvary.*
> WILLIAM R. NEWELL, "AT CALVARY"
> (1895)

Discussion Questions

1. What role do the Ten Commandments have in a discussion about eternal life?
2. How did you learn that you were a sinner?
3. What can we learn from Paul's conversion about how God saves sinners?
4. Can God save people who are very evil?

NOTES

_____

_____

_____

_____

_____

_____

_____

_____

_____

_____

_____

_____

_____

_____

_____

NOTES

NOTES

NOTES

NOTES

_____

_____

_____

_____

_____

_____

_____

_____

_____

_____

_____

_____

_____

_____

_____

_____

NOTES

_____

_____

_____

_____

_____

_____

_____

_____

_____

_____

_____

_____

_____

_____

_____

_____

NOTES

NOTES

_____

_____

_____

_____

_____

_____

_____

_____

_____

_____

_____

_____

_____

_____

_____

_____

Bible Reference for Everyday Use:

QuickNotes Simplified Bible Commentary Series

OLD TESTAMENT

*Volume 1: Genesis
thru Numbers*
978-1-59789-767-9

*Volume 2: Deuteronomy
thru Ruth*
978-1-59789-768-6

*Volume 3: 1 Samuel
thru 2 Kings*
978-1-59789-769-3

*Volume 4: 1 Chronicles
thru Job*
978-1-59789-770-9

*Volume 5: Psalms thru
Song of Solomon*
978-1-59789-771-6

Volume 6: Isaiah thru Ezekiel
978-1-59789-772-3

Volume 7: Daniel thru Malachi
978-1-59789-773-0

NEW TESTAMENT

Volume 8: Matthew and Mark
978-1-59789-774-7

Volume 9: Luke and John
978-1-59789-775-4

*Volume 10: Acts
thru 2 Corinthians*
978-1-59789-776-1

*Volume 11: Galatians
thru Philemon*
978-1-59789-777-8

*Volume 12: Hebrews
thru Revelation*
978-1-59789-778-5

Available wherever books are sold.